40 Days of God's Kingdom

40 Days of God's Kingdom

*"After his death, Jesus presented himself alive to the disciples in many different settings over a period of **forty days**. In face-to-face meetings, he talked to them about things concerning **the kingdom of God**."* Acts 1:3 (The Message)

Get God's kingdom—it's worth selling everything for!

Rick Stinton

Unless noted otherwise, Scripture quotations are taken from the Holy Bible, New International Version®, NIV® Copyright © 1973, 1978, 1984, 2011 by Biblica, Inc.® Used by permission. All rights reserved worldwide.
Scripture quotations labeled The Message are from The Message by Eugene Peterson, copyright © 1993, 1994, 1995, 2000, 2001, 2002. Used by permission of NavPress Publishing Group. All rights reserved.

Dedication

To Arthur Stinton,
now in the presence of King Jesus,
and Margaret Stinton.
You gave your children life's greatest gifts: you loved each other,
you loved us, and you showed us a genuine love for the Lord Jesus.
Your lives made it appealing for us to follow him.

———∞∞∞———

Foreword

40 Days of God's Kingdom presents an excellent guide to God's reign revealed in the Bible. The book is comprehensive yet concise. Clear and creative. Insightful and inspiring. Take the message to heart, and it will lead you to encounter heaven's loving King.

Bruce Waltke
Professor Emeritus in Old Testament Studies
Regent College

Praise for 40 Days of God's Kingdom

When God's kingdom comes into our family, our job and our church, life is SO much better! This resource will give you a greater understanding of God's kingdom, and more importantly, how to experience it daily. Through biblical teaching and practical application, Rick unpacks the mystery so we can enjoy God's kingdom invading our everyday life.

—Dave Barr, senior pastor, New Hope Windward

Healthy kingdom theology is necessary to develop fully devoted and fruitful followers of the King, Jesus. Pastor Rick's exposition is not just sound doctrine, but also a very practical teaching tool for any ministry that is committed to advancing the kingdom of God. Highly recommended.

—Fernando Castillo, senior pastor, C4 Church
Supervisor of the Hawaii District of Foursquare Churches

This 40 day study is an insightful resource that relates to the kingdom of God. Get ready for great joy as you discover more about God's rule.

—Wayne Cordeiro, senior pastor, New Hope Christian Fellowship Oahu, founder of the New Hope movement of churches

Rick has offered a remarkable and refreshing look at the heart of God's Kingdom. The book is especially helpful for churches looking for insights into the "big idea" of the Bible. Readers will discover how God's rule in our life can be experienced in new and profound ways. This helpful journey across the Bible from Creation to Revelation can only come from someone totally in love with God through Jesus Christ, deeply experienced in pastoral ministry, and extraordinarily gifted as a teacher of God's Word. I highly recommend it as a resource for building faith in diverse settings in the church.

—Randy Furushima, executive dean, Pacific Rim Christian University

Studying a part of Scripture is a wonderful blessing. But, if we don't see that passage in light of God's complete message in Scripture, it becomes like watching a video highlight without understanding where it fits in the flow of the game. My friend, Rick Stinton, has provided a very helpful and concise way to see the whole of the Bible's story, so each part can make its own special contribution. I highly recommend it.

—Gary Inrig, senior pastor emeritus, Trinity Church Redlands

Just like the two disciples on the road to Emmaus had their eyes opened to the Scriptures, so this book will help you see how Jesus is revealed in all of the Bible. It will encourage your heart to love him, and challenge you to live ready for the King's return. I urge you to read it, and study it with your small group.

—Mike Kai, senior pastor, Inspire Church

This short book is both powerful and practical. A timely read that will enable you to understand the Bible like you never have before. Great insight coupled with thought provoking questions in the Study Guide make it the perfect tool for any Bible study!

—Mike Lwin, senior pastor, New Hope Leeward

Jesus taught that the kingdom of God has come near to men. Sadly, we don't hear much preaching about the kingdom today. Pastors, including myself, seem to have forgotten the implications of the nearness of the kingdom to every individual. Rick helps remedy the situation with this refreshing book. Fun to read and full of life, this is a keeper.

—Ralph Moore, senior pastor, Hope Chapel Kahala,
founder of the Hope Chapel movement of churches

Acknowledgments

With deep gratitude to Martha, my lover and life partner in the adventure of serving King Jesus. Steve, Will, Mark and Meighan and Esther, Eric and Andrea—what treasures from God you are!

Bruce Waltke, the way you have loved God with your mind and your strength and your heart have been a life-long inspiration.

Gary and Elizabeth Inrig, you devoted yourselves to the Lord Jesus, showed me what pastors look like, led a kingdom breakout at Bethany Chapel, and fanned into flame the passion the Holy Spirit planted in me.

Darrell Bock, John Grassmick, Howard Hendricks, Bill Lawrence, John Reed, Allen Ross, and Don Sunukjian: I'm sure you have no idea what an investment you made in my life at Dallas Seminary.

Last, but not least, to my church family at New Hope Kailua: What a joy it is to advance Christ's kingdom with you! You fill my sail. And to the broader team of friends and colleagues in the New Hope movement, I'm grateful to do church as God's kingdom with you.

Table of Contents

Introduction

Imagine hiking in the woods on a beautiful, sunny day. As you walk down the trail, you notice a big, rusty can sticking out of the ground. You dig it up, and it's packed with gold coins. Millions of dollars buried in a bucket! Finders, keepers!

How would you feel? I'll tell you how I'd feel: I'd feel excited! I'd feel exhilarated! I'd burst out in the "Hallelujah Chorus."

This situation actually happened to a couple in California.[1] They were walking in the woods on a fine summer day and stumbled upon hidden treasure, mint condition gold coins from the gold rush days. Ten million dollars' worth! You can be sure that a wave of joy surged over them. But they also experienced another thing: huge change in their lives. They discovered something of immense value and their lives would never be the same.

Finding buried riches will make your heart start pumping. That's why Jesus compares hidden treasure to—get ready for this—"the kingdom of God."

> The kingdom of heaven[2] is like **treasure hidden in a field**. When a man found it, he hid it again, and then in his joy went and sold all he had and bought that field. Again, the kingdom of heaven is like a

merchant looking for fine pearls. When he found one of great value, he went away and sold everything he had and bought it.[3]

Jesus envisions that discovering God's kingdom will inspire two things: exhilarating joy, and huge change in your life. But his stories emphasize another truth, the **supreme value** of God's kingdom. It's worth selling everything for: the house, the car—OK, not the wife and kids! But definitely the gold coins, the jewelry, the artwork. Liquidate everything you own, because the kingdom of God soars beyond bucks. Even billions of them! Bill Gates would be wise to cash in. It's the deal of a lifetime.

When you find the kingdom of God, your life will be joyfully changed... forever!

What is "the kingdom of God?"

So what is "the kingdom of God?" What is Jesus saying is worth selling everything for? That's a great question.

The Scriptures show that the kingdom of God is a precious jewel with many facets. It is, at the same time, a present display of God's power on Earth shown in Jesus's miracles,[4] and yet a future event waiting his return.[5] It consists of inner spiritual qualities such as righteousness, peace, and joy.[6] Yet it encompasses Christ's rule over the nations.[7]

The key to unlocking this complexity is to realize that the biblical term conveys, at its core, a dynamic concept. The kingdom of God essentially means **God's active rule**.[8] We may get confused here, because we use the word "kingdom" in the English language in a passive sense, to describe a political territory with specified borders. In the South Pacific, for example, the Kingdom of Tonga is a defined geographical region governed by a king. The biblical meaning, however, emphasizes the authoritative exercise of ruling. This idea is best captured by action words such as "dominion" or "reign."

God's kingdom is his active, dynamic rule. It includes his authority as King, his activity of ruling as King, and the realm of his rule, including its benefits.[9]

God's kingdom, as it is used in the Bible, describes the power of God, King of the universe, actively breaking into people's lives. The exercise of his reign on Earth shows up in a number of ways. It may be the nation of Israel, a people living in the Promised Land with the LORD as their King. It may be Jesus's demonstration of power doing miracles. It may be the church, with people delivered out of Satan's domain into Jesus's reign. His kingdom. It may be the benefits of Christ's presence and rule in our lives: righteousness, peace, and joy. It may be Christ's future rule over the New Creation. All of these are facets of his kingship, his active reign breaking into history and into people's lives.

A helpful distinction to observe in the Bible is that two aspects of God's kingdom are revealed: his universal kingdom and his particular kingdom.[10] God's universal kingdom is his authority as All-powerful Creator and Sovereign King to exercise rule over all things. His universal rule is invincible and absolute.[11] God's particular kingdom, on the other hand, is his active rule breaking into the lives of people who rebelled against him, and who then came under Satan's dominion. This latter aspect of God's kingdom will be our focus.

So when Jesus tells parables about God's kingdom, he describes various aspects of God's active reign breaking into people's lives. With this insight in mind, here are three observations that will highlight the crucial importance of the kingdom of God.

First, *the kingdom of God summarizes Jesus's entire ministry.* Jesus initiates his public activity by announcing that the kingdom of God has arrived, and by calling people to receive God's rule by turning to him in faith. "The kingdom of God has drawn near. Repent and believe the good news!"[12] This isn't just one element of Jesus's teaching; it's a full summary of all his words and works. In a later chapter, we'll show how Jesus's entire ministry will invade Earth with God's rule in a profound and powerful new way.

The second observation is that ***the curriculum of Resurrection Graduate School (RGS) is the kingdom of God.*** For three years, Jesus explains and displays the kingdom of God to his disciples, inspiring their undergraduate work. When Jesus rises from the dead, guess what he teaches them at graduate school? You got it: the kingdom of God.

> After his suffering, he presented himself to them and gave many con-vincing proofs that he was alive. He appeared to them over a period of forty days and ***spoke about the kingdom of God.***[13]

I would have loved to enroll in RGS for that class—a 40-day intensive study of God's kingdom, with the professor being none other than the glorified King! Don't you wish Peter, John, and their classmates would have taken notes on those lectures and posted them on Facebook? Well, maybe they did, in a way. Their New Testament writings surely relay inspiration from their schooling at RGS.

In any case, I encourage you to take the journey "40 Days of God's Kingdom," using this book as a guide. If our studies accurately reflect the revelation of God's Word (you can be the Berean church,[14] check out the Scriptures for yourself, and make the call), we'll surely track closely with Jesus's kingdom messages at RGS. After all, he wrote the textbook![15]

That leads to our final observation. ***The kingdom of God is the primary theme of the Bible.*** If that's a new idea for you, I hope to persuade you of it by the time you finish reading these pages. For now, let me support the claim by considering the "big idea"[16] of the Bible.

What is the "Big Idea" of the Bible?

What would you say, in a sentence, is the message of the Bible? Some would answer "The Bible tells us about God and salvation." True, but vague. We need a more specific summary. Others would say, "God loves you and has a wonderful plan for your life." Again, true, but incomplete. It's certainly an encouraging truth you can count on, but the Bible says a lot more than that.

Many would answer with John 3:16, a classic verse that surely summarizes the message of the Bible (that's why you see it held up in end zones at football games). "For God so loved the world that he gave his one and only Son, that whoever believes in him shall not perish but have eternal life." Better, but still not a bull's eye. Personal salvation is a vital part of the Bible's message, but as we'll see, it's one component of a bigger picture.

I've already tipped my hand concerning the big idea of the Bible. It relates to the kingdom of God. Let me state it as concisely and completely as I can. The remainder of the book will be devoted to elaborating on this idea. The message of the Bible: ***The Righteous, Loving Creator of the universe reestablishes his life-giving rule over a rebellious world cursed by sin and death.***

More specifically:

God reclaims his righteous, loving rule over a rebellious world through his Anointed King, Jesus, who

- **triumphs over Satan's evil on the cross,**
- **rescues, in supreme love, people under the curse of sin and death,**
- **and fashions a magnificent New Creation under his reign, to the praise of his glorious grace!**

Now you may be thinking that single sentence is more of a paragraph! Yep. But it's a challenge to summarize sixty-six books in one sentence, with some level of specificity.

One way to see this big idea is to consider the following simple and symmetrical outline of the Bible.

Genesis 1–2	Genesis 3 through Revelation 19	Revelation 21–22
God creates his perfect kingdom in creation	God's kingdom is ruined by rebellion and reclaimed through King Jesus	God creates his greater kingdom in the New Creation

The first two chapters of the Bible record God's exercise of perfect rule when he creates a pristine kingdom on Earth. The final two chapters of the Bible record God fashioning a New Creation, more magnificent than the first, under his righteous, life-giving rule. The intervening chapters (count 'em, 1,185!) narrate the revolt in God's kingdom, and how he works on Earth to reclaim his loving rule through his Anointed King, Jesus.

Jesus is central to the Scriptures. The entire Old Testament anticipates the arrival of God's Anointed King on Earth.[17] The New Testament records King Jesus's triumph over Satan's evil through the cross,[18] his act of supreme love to rescue rebels under the curse of sin and death (that's the personal salvation part),[19] and his return at any moment to renew the entire universe and reign over the New Creation.[20] The whole venture displays God's powerful love, his sheer goodness, and his undeserved favor. So we borrow from the insightful apostle to conclude the big idea of the Bible, "to the praise of his glorious grace!"[21] When you realize the wonder of God's kingdom, you'll be filled with adoration for the Loving King.

I Have a Dream

As we set off together, my prayer for you is three-fold. First, that you would gain a greater understanding of the "big picture" of the Bible. As we consider the various parts, and how they relate to the whole, I pray that you'll come to appreciate more fully the spectacular panorama of God's Word. This will happen as you devote your mind to learning God's revelation over the 40 days. This book is designed as a brief overview to help you, sort of like a concise tourist guide, or the Bible's Cliffs Notes. The goal is to read and study one chapter a week, for seven weeks. They're short chapters, but loaded.

Second, I hope that you'll grow in your personal experience of God's kingdom. That God's rule will invade your life in new and deeper ways. That King Jesus will capture your heart more fully with his loving reign. Kingdom growth will emerge as you apply the King's Word, practically and personally, to the particulars of your life. Our Study Guide will show you the way. You can also fast forward to the Conclusion to read seven kingdom keys, or essential ways to engage Christ's reign. But get ready for great joy! As we shall see throughout Scripture: where God rules, he reigns with favor.

My third hope, and confident expectation, is that by walking the 40 Days with Jesus, you'll grow in your awe for our Loving King. You'll respond to him with adoration worthy of His Majesty. This will happen as you seek him in heart-to-heart encounters. Our Study Guide, again, will coach you in this vital aspect of the journey.

The goal? Simply to love him with all your mind, with all your strength, and with all your heart. To sing with the angels,

Hallelujah!
For our Lord God Almighty Reigns.
Let us rejoice and be glad and give him glory! [22]

Chapter One

Genesis 1–11

The Creator King's Majestic Rule on Earth is Ruined by Rebellion

Let the adventure begin! The first movement in the symphony of God's kingdom is a beautiful harmony. But it soon crashes into a tragedy, a clanging clamor of rebellion. Here's an overview of the events.

A Snapshot of Genesis 1–11

The Sovereign, Life-Giving King of the universe creates his majestic kingdom on Earth,

- **but his loving rule is ruined by human rebellion,**
- **and the curse of sin and death spreads over the planet.**

Majesty

Kingdom Created

The opening scene of the Bible presents a Majestic King who creates a magnificent kingdom on Earth. The Creator King issues a series of royal decrees. In response, a place of chaos is progressively transformed into a structured cosmos, an ordered planet flourishing with life. The King's sovereign commands birth the universe. His power is breathtaking, his majesty unrivalled, and his goodness absolute.

At the crown of creation, the Loving King fashions two creatures with a distinctive dignity, bearing his image on Earth.[23] A prince and a princess! They are *personal*, uniquely endowed with the capacity to experience loving relationships, with their King and with each other. And they are *royal*, gifted with the ability to exercise the Powerful King's rule over his creation kingdom.

Genesis 1:1–2:3 presents a masterful portrait of God creating his kingdom on Earth. The literary beauty of the passage can only be appreciated by viewing its symmetry and parallel structure. Consider the outline of the creation account in Chart 1.[24]

Chart 1: The Creation Account, Genesis 1:1–2:3

Title (1:1)
Summary Statement: "God created the universe"

Conditions of Chaos (1:2a)
1. formlessness
2. emptiness
3. darkness over the deep

Anticipation of the Sovereign King's Creative Work (1:2b)
The Spirit of God hovers over the waters

The Loving King Creates the Universe by Royal Decree (1:3–31)

A. God Creates Order (1:3–13)
[overcomes darkness and formlessness]

B. God Fills the Order (1:14–31)
[overcomes emptiness]

DAY 1: light from darkness

DAY 4: sun/moon for day/night

DAY 2: sea and sky

DAY 5: creatures for sea and sky

DAY 3: sea and fertile land/vegetation

DAY 6: creatures for fertile land
Climax: majesty of man and woman

Conclusion (2:1–3)

DAY 7: Sabbath: the Holy King rests from his creative work; he sets his kingdom apart for his loving rule of righteousness and life

The first chapter of Genesis begins with a title summarizing the account of creation. In the beginning, God creates "the heavens and the earth," the Hebrew expression for the universe. The scene starts with a description of three conditions of chaos: formlessness, emptiness, and darkness over deep waters. These elements of anarchy are contrary to the Loving King's reign. Over creation week, he systematically conquers them, overruling chaos and fashioning a beautiful, ordered planet thriving with life.

Consider carefully the work of the Creator King, and you'll be amazed at the magnificence of his conquering power. On the first three creation days, he triumphs over two conditions of chaos, darkness, and formlessness. On Day 1, the King conquers darkness with a royal decree speaking light into existence. He overrules formlessness by creating order in time, separating the light from the darkness, and calling them day and night. On Day 2, he further triumphs over formlessness by creating order in space. His royal edict separates sky above and sea below. On Day 3, he overcomes formlessness one more time by creating more order in space. He commands the separation of sea from fertile land. So in the first three days, the Creator King conquers two conditions of chaos, darkness and formlessness, by sovereign decree.

After three creation days, God has created order on the planet, but it remains barren. There's no life. On the next three creation days, the Loving King conquers the final condition of chaos, emptiness. He triumphs by filling the created structure with teeming life. Note the parallelism between the days. Days 1 and 4 go together: God fills the realm of time with heavenly lights to govern the seasons, years, day, and night. Days 2 and 5 match up: God invigorates the sea and sky with swimming marine life and soaring birds. Days 3 and 6 harmonize: God animates the fertile Earth with hordes of land creatures.

The Loving Creator saves his best for last, though. At the crown of creation, he fashions the man and the woman uniquely in his image. Adam and Eve are designed to know his love, and to exercise his rule over a magnificent kingdom.

Don't miss the significance of this final act in the creation drama. God is the Loving King of the universe. He triumphs over the elements of anarchy and establishes his majestic kingdom on Earth. He creates an ordered planet flourishing with life. Then, in the climactic scene, he uniquely fashions one couple to have a relationship with him and with each other. He creates us to love us, and for us to love one another. He is the Sovereign, Life-Giving King. We are his uniquely loved representatives, gifted with the ability to govern his kingdom on Earth.

Having conquered anarchy in the first six creation days and established his reign on Earth, the Loving King rests from his creative work on the seventh day. In summary, he sets his magnificent kingdom apart for his loving rule of righteousness and life.

What Kind of King is He?

The creation account paints a masterful portrait of God's creative work. Yet even more significantly, it reveals the absolute majesty of the Creator King. We have noted that he's the **Conquering King**. He triumphs over chaos to create an ordered, living planet. He makes a mess into a masterpiece. Where there is darkness and disorder, he creates light and life. What a profound glimpse into the character of the King! His recreating nature, on display in creation, will fully shine forth in his later creations, Israel and the Church.

The manner in which he creates declares he is the **Sovereign King**. He possesses unfathomable power. Awe-inspiring power! He simply speaks, and the universe obeys his command. He issues a royal decree, and the world is transformed. There is a hint here about the power of God's Word, which Israel and the Church will receive in written form. There's also a whisper of the power of God's Living Word, King Jesus, who centuries later visits our planet.[25]

In the Creator's craftsmanship, his radiant love shines forth in many rays of splendor. He is the **Life-Giving King**. He fills his kingdom with a vast variety, a swarming abundance, of living organisms. Every plant that seeds and sprouts, every animal that swims or soars or scampers, and every person who lives and loves—the King gifts all of these with life. He further grants them reproductive power to "be fruitful and multiply,"[26] surging his kingdom with life. In every sense, he is the Author of life.

He is the **Relational King**. Not a faceless force, he exists as a Person. In some mysterious way, he exhibits relationship within himself. "Let us make mankind in our image."[27] Adam and Eve are crafted as personal beings in the image of their King.[28] They are particularly gifted with the ability to enjoy intimate relationships, with their King and with each other. They can know and be known, love and be loved.

The rule of the absolutely **Good King** is also on superb display. The song of creation rings forth a continual chorus, "it is good,"[29] leading to the crescendo, "it is very good!"[30] All his works, without exception or variance, showcase his benevolence. Every detail of creation is an expression of the sheer goodness of the King.

He is the **Creative King** and the **Generous King**. His creation overflows with inspiring beauty and infinite creativity. No longer in its pristine condition, the planet still declares the King's genius for all to see.[31] (If you doubt this truth, just leave Kansas and visit Hawaii.) The King's generosity is highlighted by the abundance of beautiful trees providing delicious fruit for his specially loved image bearers, all to be enjoyed in their lush garden paradise.[32]

He is the **Family King**. He fills his kingdom with every good gift. Yet his loving heart is on supreme display in the gift of marriage, the centerpiece of loyal love.[33] The Creator presides over a ceremony in paradise, the wedding of a man and a woman perfectly suited for each other. The couple will give each other joyful companionship, partnership in service, and pleasurable intimacy. Devoted to each other in self-giving love, they will share life together at its deepest levels, naked and unashamed. The beauty of their marriage is entirely a gift from the heart of their Loving King.

A summary of all his majestic attributes is that he is the **Holy King**. Incomparable! The Loving Creator is separate from his creation. He towers above it. Indeed, the entire universe is set apart by his Word to his purposes. He especially makes the seventh day holy, a reflection of himself. The completed works of the Loving King declare that he is absolute in power, perfect in purity. He rules in righteousness and life.

Mutiny

What is the first act in the Bible? A Majestic King creates a pristine kingdom on Earth. A newlywed couple begins their honeymoon, fully alive to God and fully in love with each other. It's heaven on Earth! Adam and Eve are given one command in paradise. Amid the King's bountiful generosity, one fruit is forbidden, for their protection and good. Obeying the Loving King's decree indicates their trust and loyalty.[34] From the very beginning, keeping his Word is the means by which you respond to his love, enjoy his favor, and affirm his kingship.[35]

What starts as superb harmony in God's kingdom, however, crashes into discord. In the tragedy of all time, the prince and princess choose mutiny over loyalty.[36] Eve listens to the serpent's spin, subtle and sinister. Do you hear his hiss? "The King doesn't really have your best interests in mind. He's holding out on you. He doesn't truly love you." She buys the lie and doubts the goodness of her King. Eve bites into the serpent's treachery; Adam directly defies his Loving King.

By disobeying their King's caring command, Adam and Eve plunge paradise into pain. They reject God's majestic reign and take sides with the serpent, whose word they choose to follow. The Creator King's perfect rule on Earth is broken, and the first family surrenders to the devil's dominion.[37] Rebellion results in ruin. It's a tragedy of the first order.

The Fall Out of the Fall

The Word of the Life-Giving King proves to be true…you must not eat from the tree of the knowledge of good and evil, for when you eat from it you will certainly die.[38] The couple's defiance of his one loving command brings death into the world. Disobedience opens the door to the morgue. But the fall out of the fall shows that more than physical death is at stake.

The rebellion in God's kingdom on Earth results in two major catastrophes.[39] First, relationships are ruined. Adam and Eve's exquisite gift of a relationship with their Creator, whose image they bear, fractures. The prince and princess's intimacy with their Loving King collapses into separation, shame, fear, and guilt. Simultaneously, the loving harmony the couple enjoyed with each other fractures into self-centeredness, insecurity, hostility, and blame. Death slithers in and poisons what had been a pristine realm of relationships.

The second major fall out of the fall is that God dispenses his judgment. Along with his other excellent attributes on display in creation, we now see that the Creator King rules with justice. Penalties that fit the crime are decreed to all guilty parties. First, the serpent is cursed. The evil one, who slanders the Good King and deceives Eve into death, will eat the food of death.[40] God's enemy, who seduces the woman into an act of hostility against her Loving King, will suffer perpetual hostility with the woman's offspring. But the battle will end decisively when a descendant of Eve will crush the serpent's head in ultimate defeat. The instigator of ruin in God's kingdom will come to final ruin, at the hand of a son of the loved one who was deceived into ruin. Justice will be served.

The Just King speaks judgment, secondly, to the woman. Because she despised her relationship with him, she'll now suffer pain in relationships. In the unique gift given her of child bearing, she'll endure physical pain in giving birth, as well as relational pain in raising her children. Her relationship with her husband also suffers damage. In their fallen state, harmonious love will be infected with conflict and domination.

The Righteous King next speaks judgment on the man for his rebellion. His act of hostility, spoiling God's pristine kingdom, will be met with the good Earth's hostility toward him. Through painful toil and sweat he will labor for a living, until the day of death arrives and he returns to the substance from which he was made.

In summary, the Loving King's magnificent kingdom on Earth is ruined by the sin of rebellion. The couple, upon whom he particularly set his affection, betray his love and commit mutiny. Pain infiltrates paradise. Rewarding relationships and flourishing life plunge into brokenness and death. The good Earth itself suffers bondage to death.[41] In every way, the curse of evil poisons the pristine planet.

Glimmers of Hope amid the Disaster

Genesis 3 records the heartbreaking tragedy that ruins God's kingdom on Earth. The disastrous scene, however, concludes with glimmers of hope. The Sovereign, Life-Giving King is never taken by surprise. Even in judgment, as we see for the first time in this passage, there is hope for humanity. The Powerful King who rules with justice is, at the same time, the God of all grace. Glimmers of hope anticipate that his reign of life and love will ultimately prevail.

The first ray of hope is that, surrounded by the onslaught of death, Adam chooses a name for his wife that foresees life.[42] Eve will be the mother of all living, and the echo of God's Word is that her offspring will one day crush the enemy.[43] The King's decree inspires hope that a son of Eve will conquer the evil one, under whose realm of disobedience and death the King's loved ones have been taken captive.

The second hint of hope amid disaster is God's provision of clothing for the naked and ashamed rebels.[44] The gift of skin garments signifies the death of animals to supply their needs. This is the first glimpse of what the Just King provides in Israel's later history. He grants the substitutionary sacrifice of animals to meet the spiritual needs of people under the curse of sin. This, of course, was itself a foreshadowing of the one effective sacrifice, King Jesus's death on the cross, which provides forgiveness of sins for all rebels.[45] So in the Loving King's gracious gift of animal skins, we gain an initial glimpse of hope into his loving provision for sinners.

A third glimmer of hope in the chapter is Adam and Eve's banishment from the Garden.[46] Though at first this may seem an additional punishment, it was graciously designed to prevent them from eating from the tree of life and suffering an eternal existence in their painful, corrupted condition.

The Downward Spiral

If the ruin of God's magnificent kingdom on Earth, with its devastating results, isn't bad enough, the history of early civilization shows it gets worse. The firstborn son of Eve, mother of all the living, inflicts death on his brother.[47] Cain follows the serpent's lead of attacking the Creator King by assaulting a person bearing his image, but now with deadly violence. Cain's descendent, Lamech, takes rebellion to new depths by rejecting the Loving King's design for marriage and by proudly boasting about destroying God's image bearer.[48]

The subsequent genealogy beats with a rhythm of one gruesome reality for Adam's family: death reigns.[49] A menacing epitaph hangs over every person's life: "and then he died." It's a perpetual reminder of the disastrous loss of the Creator's life-giving rule on Earth. The notable exception is Enoch, who escapes the death sentence only by God's extraordinary intervention.[50] Enoch walks with God, and it seems that the Sovereign King enjoys the relationship so much he decides to overrule death row and take his friend home. Such a unique experience hearkens back to the Good King's original purpose for creating people, to love them. It further provides a ray of hope that fallen sons of men may live in friendship with their Loving King.

This glimpse of hope that Enoch provides, however, is overwhelmed by dark shadows of depravity in history's next chapter.[51] The human race degenerates to such depths of continual evil that the Righteous King is overcome with grief. The creatures he fashioned from an immensely loving heart reject his rule so thoroughly they are dominated by wickedness. "Every inclination of the thoughts of the human heart was only evil all the time."[52] The Creator King's once joyful heart is now filled with pain. There is only one thing to do. Turn back the ordered waters of creation to their original state of chaos and destroy evil in a flood of judgment. The utter rebellion must be brought to an end.

It's only an act of the Loving King's grace amid his grief and pain that spares Noah and his family from the waters of destruction.[53] You would hope that the new humanity that emerges from the flood, blessed once more and granted an eternal covenant,[54] would make a fresh start on Earth. You would hope that the new first family, delivered from death and favored to live under a colorful rainbow of their Saving King's grace, would set a new course for the human race and leave a new legacy. Sadly, history shows they carry their forefather's DNA of depravity. Noah lies in the new world drunk and naked. His son dishonors him, and Noah pronounces a curse on his grandson. Canaan will be the poster child for immorality.[55] Further family members of the new world, stirred by immense pride, rise up in unified rebellion against their Creator. Heaven's King responds to the revolt on Earth by acting in judgment to confuse their language and scatter them across the world.[56]

Do you hear the music? God orchestrates a majestic symphony in creating his kingdom on Earth, but it crashes into a clamoring discord—a rebellious babble echoing across the planet.

A Snapshot of Early Civilization

What does Genesis 3–11 record about the history of God's kingdom on Earth?

The Loving King's majestic rule on Earth is ruined

- **by the initial sin of human rebellion,**
  which brings the reign of death into the world,
- **and the further degeneration of humanity**
  in prideful disobedience to the Good King's rule.

By all accounts, God's kingdom on Earth is defeated. Though the planet is birthed in majesty and life, evil infiltrates and dominates. The serpent's treachery successfully triggers rebellion. Death and disorder invade and pervade. The Creator King's image bearers degenerate to such depths they must be destroyed in judgment. Even then, the new humanity emerging in the cleansed new world, saved by the Loving King's grace, continues its defiant ways. The cancer of rebellion spreads across the planet. The serpent is winning. The kingdom of the Loving, Life-Giving King is overthrown.

Or is it? The downward spiral of depravity on the planet and the apparent defeat of God's kingdom set the stage for D-Day on Earth. The Conquering King is about to invade. Against the darkest of backdrops, he does his best work.

Chapter Two

Genesis 12 through Deuteronomy

The Loving King Creates Israel
as a Base of His Rule on a Rebellious Planet

D-Day on Planet Earth

June 6, 1944. "D-Day" stands as the greatest military invasion in human history. Under the command of General Dwight D. Eisenhower, 200,000 troops storm a fifty-mile stretch of beach at Normandy, France. Allied forces deploy 12,000 aircraft and a naval armada of 7,000 vessels, including 1,200 warships. The massive invasion achieves a strategic victory, a turning point for the Allies in winning World War II.

The significance of D-Day is that the Allied armies gained a beachhead in Europe. Previously, Adolf Hitler, the evil commander of Nazi Germany, had overrun the region. But D-Day was a decisive invasion that gained a foothold on the continent. Once rooted on European soil, the Allies would fight to liberate people and nations from the tyranny of the Nazi Regime. D-Day was the beginning of the end for Hitler and his war machine. Less than a year later, on May 7, 1945, his evil reign was over and World War II ended in Europe with Allied victory.

A Spiritual Invasion

The physical invasion of D-Day provides insight for the spiritual invasion record-ed in the Pentateuch, the first five books of the Bible. Genesis 3–11 reports how Satan's rule overran the planet. He is the evil prince, the spirit ruler leading a dis-obedient kingdom worldwide against the Loving King.[57] Humanity resides in his realm, under the curse of death. Each person born on Earth is birthed into the re-bellion; each person also willingly participates. The lethal result is that everyone is taken captive by Satan's deceitful power. Whether they realize it or not, all people are in desperate need of being set free from his dominion of death.

With this scene in mind, Genesis 12 is a pivotal chapter in God's Word. Just as the Allies invaded Normandy to gain a foothold in Europe, in Genesis 12 the Conquering King invades planet Earth to gain a beachhead for his loving rule in enemy territory. The LORD initiates a relationship with Abraham. He sets his love on a family, through whom he will build a nation. Israel will become a theocracy, the deeply loved kingdom of God on Earth. They will become a treasured people over whom the LORD rules, residing in a specific territory granted them by Heaven's King.

God sets his heart of love on Israel in order to gain a foothold of his reign on Earth. He establishes a base of operations, if you will, through whom he will work to advance his life-giving strategy on enemy ground. Planet Earth had been overrun by the dominion of death. Through the spiritual base of Israel, the Conquering King will ultimately work to reclaim his righteous rule over the rebellious world. He will defeat the evil serpent and triumph over the curse of sin and death. He will liberate rebel captives whom he loves from Satan's domain of darkness. He will ultimately reestablish his righteous, life-giving rule over the entire planet. The Loving King will completely prevail!

It all begins with the invasion of Genesis 12. That's why it's such a pivotal chapter. It's the first step in the King's conquest, the beginning of the end of the serpent's dominion. The first five books of the Bible, starting with

Genesis 12, narrate the creation of Israel as God's deeply loved kingdom on Earth.

Here's a quick description of this foundational section of Scripture:

A Snapshot of Genesis 12 through Deuteronomy

The Creator King breaks into a rebellious world to form Israel as his treasured kingdom on Earth,

- **in a committed, loving relationship with him,**
- **to represent his righteous rule,**
- **with the ultimate purpose of triumphing over the curse of death and giving life to all peoples of the world.**

I know, another sentence paragraph. But give me a break. Those are five long books! Each book will be considered briefly, to see how they contribute to this overarching idea. God invades history to create the covenant nation of Israel, his dearly loved kingdom on Earth.

Genesis

The first book of the Bible reveals God creating his majestic kingdom on Earth (Chapters 1–2), followed by its ruin and the spread of evil (Chapters 3–11). But the majority of the book (Chapters 12–50) recounts the Loving King setting his love on Abraham and his family in a covenant relationship. God's treasured kingdom on Earth originates in the family of Abraham. The actual nation of Israel is birthed in the events recorded in Exodus. But the family roots of God's kingdom are in the great Patriarch.

God's call of Abraham in Genesis 12 is the turning point. The Life-Giving King breaks into history to establish a committed, loving relationship with Abraham and his family. He makes three covenant promises to Abraham:[58] 1) to bless him and make him a great nation; 2) to give him the land of Canaan; and 3) through him to bless all the peoples of the Earth. All three promises possess huge significance, but don't miss the last one. When God "blesses," it means something much more profound than wishing that you "have a nice day." It means the Life-Giving King of the universe fills you with the potency of life.[59] In the context of Genesis, it declares triumph over the curse of death that poisoned his reign. God's loving purpose through Abraham was to infuse people of all nations with life.[60] This ultimately leads to the arrival of King Jesus on Earth, with his mission of granting life in its fullest measure.[61]

The fact that the King makes a covenant with Abraham is also rich with significance. A covenant means a committed relationship, built on the twin pillars of loyalty and affection. The Loving King is drawing a family to him.[62] He commits to be their God, and he requires their faithfulness to him. At the heart of the relationship is the Covenant King's loyal love.

Abraham's response to God's call is amazing. He takes the risk of faith. He leaves everything, the comfortable life he knows, to travel to a foreign land. Going without knowing, he has no idea where he will end up or what the future will hold. He simply trusts and obeys the King's Word. (Remember the response of creation to the Word of the King?) After this initial, remarkable response of faith in the King and his promise, Abraham often falters in his trust. Yet he emerges as the father of our faith.[63] Indeed, his life models two essential truths for all people who seek to know the Loving King. First, we embrace a relationship with him by a response of faith, placing our trust in him and obeying his Word.[64] Second, the Righteous King credits our faith as righteousness.[65]

Abraham's family, through Isaac and Jacob, inherit the Covenant King's promises. Their history shows that, along with the rest of humanity, the loved covenant family carries the DNA of depravity. "Pictures" in their "photo album" display some shameful, degenerate behavior. Certain family videos are definitely not PG! Yet a vital truth emerges from their life stories and proves to be an essential feature of God's rule on Earth. ***The Loving King acts sovereignly to protect his promises.*** Whether God's vow is put at risk by personal failures within the chosen family[66] or threatened by external powers,[67] the King rules by safeguarding his promises. Despite the fickleness of people, he is the Faithful King. His royal purposes prevail.

A Snapshot of Genesis

The Creator King breaks into the rebellious world cursed by sin and death

> **by calling Abraham and his descendants into a committed, loving relationship with him, promising**

- **to bless them and make them a great nation,**
- **to give them the land of Canaan,**
- **and to give life to all peoples of the Earth through them.**

Exodus

Exodus records how the Loving King creates Israel as a theocracy, a nation under his righteous rule. Genesis concludes with Abraham's descendants living as a family clan in Egypt. How does the covenant family become the kingdom of God? Exodus tells the story.

Three primary events forge Israel into God's treasured kingdom. First, the King rescues his loved family from slavery in Egypt.[68] He sovereignly fashions a leader, Moses, to liberate his people from bondage to Egypt, the world's super power. Then, through ten powerful plagues of judgment on Egypt's false gods,[69] the Covenant King sets his people free. His mighty acts declare one decisive truth to Abraham's family and the rebellious nations of the world. He is the one true God, all-powerful Creator and King of the Universe.

In the process of recruiting Moses, the Creator King reveals himself in a new and deeply meaningful way. He gives himself a distinctive name, YHWH: "I AM WHO I AM."[70] He is self-existent and eternal. In light of Moses's insecurities, he is sovereign and all sufficient. As the Loving King moves in history to gather his people to him, he takes "I AM" (translated "LORD") as his personal covenant name. He is the relationship-seeking, promise-keeping God. He is loyalty and love in Person, rescuing his treasured people.

By the way, centuries later, Jesus of Nazareth openly refers to himself with this name, on many occasions. "I AM" the good shepherd.[71] "I AM" the way, the truth and the life.[72] "I AM" the resurrection and the life.[73] Before Abraham was born, "I AM."[74]

The second event of major significance in Exodus relates to the King's purpose for rescuing his loved people from Egypt. He makes a further covenant relationship with them at Mount Sinai.[75] Central to his covenant with Israel is the Law, a revelation of his righteous character. The Law sets the nation apart as the King's treasured people, his representatives on Earth.[76] It reveals how his family must exercise loyalty to their Loving, Rescuing King, by obeying his righteous commands. The Law also serves as a national constitution, forging Israel's identity as one nation under God, the kingdom of God on Earth.

The Covenant at Sinai reveals two dimensions of the Loving King's reign: the citizens' love for God and their love for people.[77] On the vertical plane, the covenant family is called to honor their Creator King in a manner worthy of His Majesty. On the horizontal plane, they are called to value fellow image bearers in every aspect of their relationships. The Loving King's reign of righteousness and compassion must be exercised toward all people, but especially in social justice toward the poor and the oppressed.

The third major event in Exodus, when you think about it, is nothing short of a scandal. God grants the Tabernacle.[78] The Holy King, who rules the universe with absolute majesty, stoops to camp in a tent, in the wilderness of Sinai! Amid a horde of runaway slaves!! Can you fathom the significance? The King who towers above creation focuses his presence, somehow, at a particular point on Earth. The place? The center of Israel's camp, in close proximity and relationship to his loved people.

The Rescuing King draws near. The Conquering King invades Satan's domain on Earth. The Loving King of the universe sets his throne in Israel's tent.

A Snapshot of Exodus

The All-Powerful King of the universe creates Israel as his loved kingdom on Earth, by

- **rescuing Abraham's family from slavery in Egypt,**
- **forging them into a covenant nation under his righteous Law,**
- **and dwelling among them in the Tabernacle.**

Leviticus

Now, did you catch the problem? How does creation's Holy King, pure and life-giving, reside among corrupted, death-cursed rebels? That may seem a harsh description of Israel, but it's accurate. (Unfortunately, it's an accurate description of you, too, apart from King Jesus. But we're getting ahead of ourselves.)

A colossal problem accompanies the Creator King's decision to live among his people. A deadly collision is imminent. The Holy King's moral purity is absolute. When he comes in contact with depravity, he acts, by nature, in judgment. Like light and darkness, the two cannot coexist. Radiant light, by its very essence, destroys darkness. God's holy presence necessarily destroys impurity. That's a huge problem, because the covenant people of Israel inherited the DNA of depravity (yeah, you and me, too).

So how can the Holy King reside among an unholy people without destroying them? The Invading King supplies the answer in Leviticus. This revelation, in concert with the design of the Tabernacle, is of supreme significance. The Loving King locates his throne in the inner sanctuary of the Tabernacle, the holiest of holy places. Note that he is described as ruling from above the mercy seat. He reigns in compassion for his people's needs. The LORD is separated from the people by a series of courtyards, for their protection, lest they come in contact with his holy presence, to their destruction.

Yet the Holy King desires to live in close relationship with his loved people, and to bless them. So in the first section of Leviticus, he shows his covenant family how they can approach him.[79] The King institutes animal sacrifices and the service of priests, who act as intermediaries between him and the people. In the animal sacrifices, the Holy King reveals a crucial spiritual solution: substitutionary atonement. It is the Gracious King's gift for the sinner to approach him, solving the deadly collision imminent when human depravity approaches divine purity.

How does it work? Well, as decreed initially in the Garden,[80] the just penalty for sin is death. However, in an act of sheer undeserved favor, the judgment of death is placed *not* on the guilty party, but on a substitute (the animal sacrificed). The Righteous King upholds justice. The price of sin is paid. The animal suffers death. With the lawbreaker's act of faith in the LORD's provision, the Gracious King releases him or her from the death penalty, which has been executed already. He declares the rebel righteous. He welcomes the forgiven sinner into his presence. What a supreme gift from the Just and Loving King!

In the second section of Leviticus, the King teaches practical matters of holy living.[81] The LORD's deeply loved people must display his character by living distinctively in a world contaminated by sin, decay, and death. Every aspect of their lives—their personal relationships, hygiene, agricultural methods, diet, and worship practices—must reflect the truth that Heaven's King rules with purity and life. Kingdom people must be holy, because their Loving King is holy.[82]

A Snapshot of Leviticus

The Holy King provides instruction for his loved, sin-contaminated people

- **to approach him through the offerings,**
- **and to live distinctive lives as his representatives on Earth,**
  so he can dwell among them and bless them.

Numbers

The Loving King adopts a family (Genesis), forges them into a nation living under his rule at Mount Sinai (Exodus), and provides a way for them to live in his presence (Leviticus). So how does the nation of Israel, formed at Mount Sinai, get to Canaan, the kingdom land granted to Abraham? I just knew you would ask!

Numbers records the kingdom of God on a road trip. It tells the story of Israel's travels from Mount Sinai to Moab, the land right next to Canaan. The journey ends with Israel camped east of the Jordan River, on the threshold of their kingdom land. The book narrates the treasured nation's organization at Mount Sinai,[83] their journey through the wilderness,[84] and preparations at the gate to the Promised Land.[85] The wonderful news about Numbers is that Israel, newly inspired by the King's awesome power and love displayed in their deliverance from Egypt, lays hold of their destiny and prospers under the rule of their Rescuing King. OK, if you believe that, you haven't read the book yet. Just checking.

Sadly, the nation's journey to their kingdom destination, which should've taken eleven days,[86] ends up taking forty years. The reason? In a word: unbelief. In five words: rejecting their Loving King's rule. There it is, again, rebellion. The journey features several failures of the kingdom people to trust their Provider King when they face challenges in the wilderness. But their unbelief comes to a climax at a crucial point at Kadesh Barnea. They fail an entrance exam to the kingdom. After experiencing their All-Powerful King liberating them from Egypt, the rescued people refuse to trust him for victory over Canaan.[87] Their disregard for their Loving King constitutes rebellion in his kingdom.

The Just King's judgment, again, fits the crime. Those who refuse to trust him to enter the kingdom land will receive what they choose. They will not enter the land. Instead, they will march around the wilderness for forty years until they die. Yet because the King rules with loyal love, he will take the next generation of Abraham's family into the Land.

In spite of Israel's tragic record on the journey, Numbers actually declares great news. Despite threats from within (rebellion and unbelief) and threats from without (nation's attacks), the King is faithful in protecting his covenant promises. The LORD's unfailing love always prevails.

Ring a bell? We saw that same dynamic of God's rule in Genesis. *Déjà vu*, all over again.

A Snapshot of Numbers

The Faithful King leads his loved kingdom from Mount Sinai to the border of the Promised Land, by

- **organizing them in the wilderness,**
- **overcoming threats from within and without on the journey,**
- **and preparing them to enter their kingdom land.**

Deuteronomy

The final book of the Pentateuch records five MP3's—**M**oses **P**reaching for the triune God (**3**). The exceptional prophet-pastor[88] pours out his heart to the congregation of Israel. His purpose:

- to renew the Covenant King's relationship of commitment and affection with the children of the wilderness rebels;
- to prepare them spiritually so they thrive as God's kingdom in Canaan;
- to inspire loyal love toward their Rescuing King.

What was the "big idea" Moses preached? The Conquering King set his loving heart on you.[89] Love him with all you've got, because he's worthy.[90] Recognize that tune? King Jesus affirms Moses's message—to love God with all of your heart, soul, mind, and strength—as the greatest thing you can do with your life.[91]

A Snapshot of Deuteronomy

The Loving King renews his relationship with the next generation of Israel

- **by calling the people to respond to his loyal love with their loving loyalty to his kingship and covenant,**
  - **in order to prepare them to enter the Promised Land of Canaan.**

Since the dawn of creation to the renewed covenant with Israel, one thing is certain: The King of the universe loves his people and seeks a loving relationship with them. As God's treasured people stand at the threshold of inheriting the real estate granted by their Loving King, how will they respond to his favor and rule? The Historical Books record the next movement in God's kingdom on Earth. They tell the story of the LORD's family living in their kingdom land.

Chapter Three

Historical Books: Joshua through Nehemiah

The Loving King Rules over Israel in Anticipation of Sending His Anointed King, Jesus

Let's review what we've learned about the foundation of God's kingdom in history before we build on it.

Snapshot Review

The "Big Idea" of the Bible

God reclaims his righteous, loving rule over a rebellious world
through his Anointed King, Jesus, who

- triumphs over Satan's evil on the cross,
- rescues, in supreme love, people under the curse of sin and death,
- and fashions a magnificent New Creation under his reign,
to the praise of his glorious grace!

Genesis 1–11

The Life-Giving King creates his majestic kingdom on Earth, but human rebellion ruins it with sin and death.

Genesis 12 through Deuteronomy

The Creator King forms Israel as his loved kingdom on Earth, in order to triumph over the curse of death and give life to all the peoples of the world.

The Pentateuch records how the LORD created Israel as his dearly loved kingdom, a base of his rule on Earth. The curtain comes down on this first act with the nation standing at the border of Canaan, yet to occupy the Promised Land. Joshua picks up the story, narrating Israel's conquest of their kingdom territory. The remainder of the Historical Books recount Israel's track record as God's kingdom, as well as developments in the Loving King's rule.

The books span a thousand years of time, from Joshua's day (about 1400 B.C.) to Nehemiah (about 400 B.C.). The Conquering King, whose loving rule has gained a foothold in enemy territory, advances his strategy in and through his covenant people. It appears that he's not in a hurry. On the other hand, much of the story features Israel's response toward her Loving King. The nation's habitual rejection of the LORD's rule plays a significant role in the slow progress of the King achieving his purposes. If Israel's history as God's kingdom on Earth were a concerto, it would reverberate with a refrain of rebellion.

Israel's family history unfolds in three major movements.[92] First, the kingdom of God rises to its high point under David (Joshua, Judges, Ruth, 1 and 2 Samuel). Then it declines, tragically, leading to the exile (1 and 2 Kings). The third movement is the restoration of God's kingdom people to the land

(Esther, Ezra, Nehemiah, 1 and 2 Chronicles). The kingdom of God is thus built, ruined, and restored.

Before we explore Israel's track record, let's view a wide-angle photo of this millennium of God's kingdom on Earth.

A Snapshot of the Historical Books (Joshua through Nehemiah)

The Covenant King exercises his loving rule in Israel's history, by

- **giving them victory to possess the Promised Land,**
- **instituting a human king to govern his reign,**
    centralizing his throne in Jerusalem
    and granting an eternal dynasty through David,
- **exiling the nation in judgment for their persistent rebellion,**
- **and restoring his loved people to their kingdom land,**
    all in anticipation of sending his Anointed King into the world.

I know, another sentence paragraph. But we're covering a thousand years of history, and twelve books!

Let's ride the three big waves of the kingdom, and then consider the strategic initiatives of God's reign in Israel.

Wave 1: The Kingdom Rises to its High Point under David

Under the capable spiritual leadership of **Joshua**, the Conquering King leads the nation and enables them to possess the kingdom land of Canaan. The renewal of the covenant at Shechem[93] affirms an essential kingdom truth: The nation's prosperity depends on the people receiving God's loving rule, shown by faithful obedience to his righteous commands.

Judges recounts the breakdown of God's kingdom into lawlessness and immorality. Israel has inherited their kingdom land and are favored to live under the Good King's reign. Yet the people abandon God's rule and sing together an ancient version of Frank Sinatra's hit, "I Did It My Way." Rather than live by the LORD's covenant, they "do what is right in their own eyes."[94] The kingdom family lapses into a pattern of repeated dysfunction: reject the King's rule, suffer oppression, cry out in distress, and then their Powerful King rescues them.[95] Over and over again, their behavior demonstrates their need for an effective spiritual leader (hint, a king), someone to unify the tribes and lead them in a faithful relationship with their Loving King.

During the Judges era of spiritual decline, the Sovereign LORD is at work behind the scenes among common people whose lives reflect his loyal love. He conquers Israel's unfaithfulness by providing a faithful spiritual leader for his kingdom on Earth. **Ruth** records the historical events in the ancestry of David, who will rise to become Israel's spiritual leader and greatest king.

1 and 2 Samuel records the dawn of a new era in the government of God's kingdom on Earth. The Creator King had previously exercised his reign through the covenant, administered by the priests. He now institutes an earthly king. Heaven's King entrusts and empowers a human king to govern his rule over the nation. The prophet, Samuel, plays a pivotal role transitioning to the new government. He anoints Israel's first two kings. But even more significantly, he defines the new order of God's rule. He initiates Israel's kingship in the framework of renewing the covenant. Israel's king is distinctively different from the kings of all other nations. The human ruler of God's kingdom on Earth is commissioned to honor Heaven's King. He is to lead the nation in faithfully serving the LORD by following his covenant.[96]

Samuel crowns Saul as the nation's first king. But Saul's disobedience to the Covenant King disqualifies him from spiritual leadership. The Sovereign King then chooses a man after his own heart to govern his kingship over Israel. David, a warrior and a worshiper, emerges as Israel's greatest king because of his loyal love for the LORD. With David administering the King's rule, Israel enjoys her greatest prosperity. He becomes the ideal, though imperfect, king.

Following David's reign, the nation's spiritual pathway winds downward, eventually leading to disaster.

Wave 2: The Kingdom Declines, Leading to the Exile

1 and 2 Kings record the decline of God's kingdom on Earth following David's reign (970 B.C.) until the Babylonian exile (586 B.C.). The inspired author narrates the nation's history from a kingdom perspective. Israel's kings are evaluated not by political or economic achievements, but by their loyalty to the LORD. The king's most essential purpose is to lead the nation in faithful relationship with their Loving King. David's reign is the standard used to measure other kings' loyalty to the LORD.

The seeds of dissension in David's family sprout after the reign of his son, Solomon, and the kingdom is divided, with Israel in the north and Judah in the south. The family history of the northern tribes is a catastrophe. Jeroboam kicks off with a game plan of idolatry, and nineteen successive kings reject God's loyal love. Each one of them does "evil in the eyes of the LORD." The human rulers governing God's reign on Earth are persistently unfaithful to their Loving King.

Note the summary of this tragic record in Chart 2.

Chart 2
A Summary of Kings Administering God's Rule over the Covenant Nation

Kings of Israel		Kings of Judah	
Jeroboam I "evil in the eyes of the LORD"		Rehoboam "evil in the eyes of the LORD"	
Nadab	"evil…"	Abijah	"evil…"
Baasha	"evil…"	Asa	"good…"
Elah	"evil…"	Jehoshophat	"good…"
Zimri	"evil…"	Jehoram	"evil…"
Omri	"evil…"	Ahaziah	"evil…"
Ahab	"evil…"	Queen Athaliah	"evil…"
Ahaziah	"evil…"	Joash	"good…"
Jehoram (Joram)	"evil…"	Amaziah	"good…"
Jehu	"evil…"	Azariah (Uzziah)	"good…"
Jehoahaz	"evil…"	Jotham	"good…"
Jehoash	"evil…"	Ahaz	"evil…"
Jeroboam II	"evil…"	Hezekiah	"good…"
Zechariah	"evil…"	Manasseh	"evil…"
Shallum	"evil…"	Amon	"evil…"
Menahem	"evil…"	Josiah	"good…"
Pekahiah	"evil…"	Jehoahaz	"evil…"
Pekah	"evil…"	Jehoiakim	"evil…"
Hoshea	"evil…"	Jehoiakin	"evil…"
		Zedekiah	"evil…"

Finally, the Patient King, who is slow to anger,[97] applies the penalty, which had been written into the covenant as a warning. The consequence of Israel's unfaithfulness is the loss of their kingdom land, through exile.[98] The Sovereign King sets his hand on Assyria, the world super power of the day, to be his instrument of judgment. Assyria invades the northern kingdom in 722 B.C. and expels the people from their covenant land. Israel's persistence in throwing off their Loving King's rule is granted. The Just King gives them over to their own way: foreign rule.

Judah's history as God's family on Earth is mixed. Eight out of twenty kings prove to be faithful spiritual leaders by doing "right in the eyes of the LORD." However, over time, Judah's continual rejection of her Loving King eventually prompts the LORD, once again, to move in judgment. This time, the Sovereign King utilizes the new world super power, Babylon, to be his instrument. Judah is destroyed and exiled in 586 B.C.

The disaster is complete. Rebellion dominates. The kingdom God had created as a base of his operations in enemy territory is destroyed. Israel's kings, who were to be governing for God, are dethroned. The LORD's throne room in the holy temple is demolished. His royal city, Jerusalem, is devastated. His loved kingdom people are displaced. The Loving King's rule on Earth is in disarray, if not defeat. Sinister Satan is smirking behind the scenes.

But the Conquering King has not surrendered the foothold of his loving rule on Earth. In the third wave of Israel's history, the LORD restores his loyally loved people to their covenant land.

Wave 3: The Kingdom People Are Restored to the Promised Land

During the disaster of the exile, the Covenant King continues to rule with loving faithfulness. **Esther** records the Sovereign King reigning in the seeming coincidences of life, with the LORD's name not even being mentioned. His chosen family is threatened with annihilation by the forces of darkness. But by saving his people from destruction, the Loving King protects the future fulfillment of his covenant promises. This is no light matter: at stake is the ultimate reclaiming of his life-giving rule on Earth through his loved people.

After the seventy years of exile announced by the King's spokesman, Jeremiah,[99] the tide begins to turn. **Ezra** and **Nehemiah** record the physical and spiritual restoration of God's treasured people to the Land. Just as Heaven's King utilized the world's super powers to carry out his purposes in judgment, so he uses the world power of Persia to restore his people to the Land. Although Israel does not achieve political independence, her renewal is complete. A representative group returns to the Land and the royal city of Jerusalem is rebuilt. The temple is reconstructed as the symbolic throne of Israel's Loving King and the center of covenant life with the LORD. Worship in the temple is revived, with sacrifices and praise, service of the priests, and annual feasts. The covenant is renewed, and the Law is reestablished in the life of the people for a loving, faithful relationship with their Restoring King.

1 and 2 Chronicles affirm the identity of the restored community as God's kingdom on Earth. The devastation of the great judgment and apparent destruction of God's kingdom had settled a haunting question among the exiled people: What is our relationship with Heaven's King? After all, the Davidic kings representing the LORD's rule had disappeared. Jerusalem, the center of God's reign, and the Temple, the focus of Israel's covenant life, had been dismantled. The people had been dispersed.

Despite all of the evidence to the contrary, the inspired author of these books declares that Israel remains God's loved kingdom on Earth. He validates their God-given passport by emphasizing their connection with three key elements of the Covenant King's loving rule: the temple in Jerusalem, the King's acts of sovereign choice, and his Word through the Law and the prophets.

The temple in Jerusalem, rebuilt by the LORD's sovereign rule exercised through the edict of the Persian King, Cyrus,[100] signifies that Israel's relationship of loyal love with her Covenant King remains. For this reason, the chronicler's account of David's and Solomon's reigns is largely devoted to David's preparation for, and Solomon's building of, the temple, as well as David's instructions for the temple service.

A second affirmation of Israel's identity as God's treasured kingdom is the chronicler's record of the King's acts of sovereign choice.[101] The LORD's various acts of election (the tribe of Levi is chosen to serve before the ark of the covenant, David is chosen to be King, Solomon is chosen to build the temple, Jerusalem is chosen to be the holy city, etc.) assure restored Israel that their rebuilt temple in Jerusalem and its continuing service mark them as the LORD's favored nation. Despite the people's unfaithfulness, the Faithful King remains committed to his kingdom on Earth. Israel's birth certificate, inscribed "the LORD's chosen family," has not been canceled.

In addition to the temple, Israel had the Law and the prophets as elements of their covenant life under the LORD's loving reign. Neither the Davidic kings nor the temple had, in themselves, assured Israel's security and prosperity. The king and the nation's blessing were based on their faithfulness to the covenant Law[102] and God's prophetic Word.

In all of these ways, the author of Chronicles assures Israel that, despite the nation's terrible track record, they are still the loved family of God. People may be unfaithful, but the Covenant King cannot deny himself. He remains faithful.

The historical books thus record the King's loving rule in Israel unfolding in three movements. The kingdom rises to a climax under David. It declines to the eventual judgment of the exile. Then the LORD's loyal love restores his chosen people to the Land.

In addition to God exercising his rule in and through his covenant nation during their history, he initiates three new developments in his kingdom. Each is birthed with profound significance.

Three New Developments in the King's Rule

The Loving King's most significant new venture, noted above, is that he institutes human kings in Israel. Moses and Joshua had demonstrated the strategic value of spiritual leaders achieving the King's purposes on Earth. The horrendous history of the Judges reaffirms this need. During Samuel's day, the people wanted a human king for the wrong reasons.[103] They wanted to be like other nations who found their security in a human leader. But the Conquering King prevails with his own purpose. When God installs anointed kings in Israel to administer his reign, he is ultimately preparing for the arrival in history of his Anointed King, Jesus.

In sharp contrast to Israel's kings, most of who did evil in the LORD's eyes, King Jesus will reign over God's kingdom with righteousness and justice. His rule will display the true majesty of our Loving King.

The King's second great initiative is that he declares a royal treaty. In response to David's loyal love, the LORD grants him a covenant, establishing his descendent as ruler over the kingdom forever.[104] This promise further anticipates the arrival of God's Anointed King on Earth. It led to the angel Gabriel's announcement to Mary at the first Christmas, describing the child she would bear. "The Lord God will give him the throne of his father David, and he will reign over Jacob's descendants forever; his kingdom will never end."[105] King Jesus, the greater Son of David, will exercise an eternal reign!

The King's third great achievement is setting up his throne in Jerusalem. David unifies the tribes and centralizes his government in the capital. Jerusalem becomes the crown city of the LORD's loving reign on Earth, and the heart of Israel's covenant life with their King. The Conquering King is preparing for his ultimate reign in the royal city, the New Jerusalem, his throne room in the New Creation.[106]

At the same time that the Loving King exercises and develops his reign in Israel's history, he actively enriches his kingdom on Earth through two other ventures. We now turn to the gift of the prophets and the poets.

⁂

Chapter Four

Prophets and Poets

The Loving King Guards His Kingdom and Reigns in Wisdom

Before we take the next step in 40 Days of God's Kingdom, let's review the road we've traveled.

Snapshot Review

The "Big Idea" of the Bible

God reclaims his righteous, loving rule over a rebellious world
through his Anointed King, Jesus, who

- triumphs over Satan's evil on the cross,
- rescues, in supreme love, people under the curse of sin and death,
- and fashions a magnificent New Creation under his reign,
    to the praise of his glorious grace!

Genesis 1–11

The Life-Giving King creates his majestic kingdom on Earth, but human rebellion ruins it with sin and death.

Genesis 12 through Deuteronomy

The Creator King forms Israel as his loved kingdom on Earth, in order to triumph over the curse of death and give life to all the peoples of the world.

Historical Books (Joshua through Nehemiah)

The Covenant King exercises his faithful rule during the highs and lows of Israel's history, all in anticipation of sending his Anointed King into the world.

The Pentateuch and the Historical Books record movements of God's kingdom unfolding, progressively, in time. First, Adam and Eve's original rebellion ruins God's majestic rule on Earth and evil spreads over the planet. God then breaks into history to create Israel as his loved kingdom, followed by his covenant rule over the nation during their history. The books of the prophets and the poets do not feature a further movement of God's kingdom unfolding in time. Rather, they record the enrichment of God's kingdom during the period of his rule over Israel. The King of the universe speaks through inspired messengers and sages to enhance his reign on Earth. The LORD has a loving purpose for both prophet and poet, and we will consider each, in turn.

A Snapshot of the Prophets (Isaiah through Malachi)

The Righteous, Loving King guards his reign through his messengers, the prophets, by

- **calling his treasured people to a faithful covenant relationship,**
- **announcing judgment for their unfaithfulness,**
- **and proclaiming the coming of his Anointed King to rule in righteousness and glory.**

The Prophet's Purpose: To Speak for the King and Guard His Rule

Since Moses's day, the King had chosen to communicate to his people through a personal spokesman, the prophet. The prophet served a vital purpose in God's kingdom: to speak God's word to his people. The importance of the King's messengers can be seen in Jehoshophat's proclamation to Israel: "Have faith in the LORD your God and you will be upheld; have faith in his prophets and you will be successful."[107] Loyalty to the Covenant King is demonstrated by faithful obedience to his Law, yet heeding the prophet's word is also crucial. Faithful kings honored the King's message through his messenger. Unfaithful kings disregarded it, to their destruction.[108]

Against the backdrop of Israel's numerous unfaithful kings, the prophets serve to guard the LORD's loving reign over his people. They are "watchmen" on the walls,[109] guardians of God's kingdom on Earth. They protect and preserve the King's rule with three essential messages. First, they plead for Israel to repent from their sin. They tell the people to turn from rejecting their Loving King's rule through the covenant, and to serve him with loyal love. The prophets speak against such sins as idolatry, immorality, hypocrisy, injustice, oppression, corruption, and so on. They urge faithfulness to the Righteous, Loving King.

The second message the prophets deliver is warning of judgment for unfaithfulness. Despite the Covenant King's loving heart for his chosen people, the King's messengers announce there will be dreadful consequences if the people continue in wickedness and rebellion. Both for Israel and Judah, as well as the rebellious nations of the world.

The message of impending judgment was not well received by a rebellious people, so the prophets often suffered rejection and violence for serving the

LORD. An unfaithful people acted out their rebellion toward their Covenant King by persecuting his messengers.

The third message the prophets deliver is more uplifting. Amid the darkness of Israel's kings continually leading the nation in doing "evil in the eyes of the LORD," the prophets shine a brilliant light of hope for the future. They announce that God's Anointed King will reign in righteousness and glory. The son of David is coming! He will exercise an eternal rule over God's kingdom, in majesty worthy of the Righteous, Loving King. The prophets speak primarily to the people and situations of their day, but a predictive element is built into their God-breathed messages. Heaven's Anointed King is coming to Earth. He is the future hope of God's kingdom!

The prophets who wrote books of the Bible may be viewed in their historical order,[110] identified by their relationship to the pivotal event of Israel's exile. Preexilic prophets speak God's Word leading up to the exile. Exilic prophets serve during the exile, and postexilic prophets serve after the exile.

The King Speaks through His Preexilic Prophets

Obadiah announces the Righteous King's judgment on Edom for its violence against his kingdom. He assures the LORD's covenant people of their deliverance and the triumph of God's rule. **Joel** calls Judah to be faithful to their covenant in light of God's coming judgment, "the day of the LORD." On that dreadful day, the nation will be judged for her unfaithfulness to her King. World nations will be judged for their treatment of his kingdom. Yet God will pour out his Spirit and salvation upon all people. The Loving King will reign from his holy throne in Jerusalem.

Jonah reminds Israel of her mission to extend the Loving King's grace to all nations, including the hated Assyrians. **Hosea** declares the King's loyal love toward his unfaithful people. Their spiritual adultery not only breaks God's Law, it breaks his heart. The prophet calls Israel to repent and receive the benefits of her Faithful King's rule. **Amos** announces that the Creator King, who rules the universe,[111] will judge his covenant-breaking kingdom on Earth. Israel's failure to practice social justice and righteousness constitutes rejection of the LORD's rule and will result in being uprooted by a foreign nation. Yet if they would change their ways, there is hope for a faithful people. Beyond the impending judgment, the Righteous King will rule again with blessing over a restored Israel, in the Promised Land, through his Davidic King. His loving reign will extend throughout the nations.

Isaiah proclaims the full dimensions of the Holy King's judgment and salvation. Israel's rebellion against his righteous rule results in awful judgment, "the day of the LORD," which will be unleashed against all nations who defy him. Yet the God of all comfort will have compassion on his kingdom people and gather them to him. His Anointed King, a descendent of David, will rule in righteousness and the nations will stream to his holy throne in Jerusalem. God's loving rule on Earth will prevail through his Righteous Ruler, the Servant of the LORD, and his righteous subjects.

Micah announces the Righteous King's judgment on his people for breaking their covenant, through idolatry, injustice, rebellion, and empty ritualism. He also declares the King's delight in their repentance. Though judgment will seem to bring the nation to an end, God's kingdom will prevail because of his covenant faithfulness. The LORD will reign with greater future glory through his Anointed King. He will rule over all the earth.

Nahum declares the Just King's judgment on Ninevah for their cruelty, idolatry, and wickedness. The Sovereign King controls the destinies of all nations, and his righteous kingdom on Earth will ultimately triumph. **Zephaniah** pronounces the Righteous King's impending judgment on "the day of the LORD," when he will punish the nations and unfaithful Judah. He calls the people to return to their King, who loves them, and who is mighty to save. His unfailing love will restore his kingdom people in their homeland and honor them among the peoples of the Earth.

Through **Habakkuk's** dialogue with the Righteous King, God reveals his judgment on Judah. Babylon will be the LORD's instrument, yet that wicked nation will also be destroyed. The prophet sets the example for God's righteous kingdom people, who must live by faith in their Savior King.

Jeremiah announces the destruction of Judah by their Just King. He will act in righteous judgment because of their stubborn rebellion and uncommitted hearts. Although it seems the LORD will undo everything he had done for his kingdom since he delivered them from Egypt, his mercy and loyal love will triumph over judgment. The kingdom will be restored after seventy years of exile and the people renewed with a new covenant. The Faithful King will write his law on their hearts. God's Anointed King from the house of David will rule in righteousness.

The King Speaks through His Exilic Prophets

Lamentations grieves the destruction of Jerusalem, the royal city from which the Holy King reigns, because of Israel's rebellion. The King's judgment prompts weeping, heartfelt remorse, and repentance among his people. Even in severe judgment, the King is recognized as the LORD of love and salvation. Great is his faithfulness.

Daniel affirms the absolute reign of the Righteous King over the kingdoms on Earth. The LORD's sovereign rule determines the destinies of the nations and also that of his kingdom, Israel. **Ezekiel** declares that the holy LORD's rule was exercised in the nation's destruction. God's kingdom had made herself unclean with defiled worship in a defiled temple, city, and land. But the Holy King is faithful, so he will revive his loved people. He will shepherd them with compassion and cleanse them from defilement. He will rebuild them as his kingdom in the covenant land, under the reign of his Davidic King. By doing so, he will display his glory among the nations and restore the glory of his presence to the holy city. The world will know that he is the LORD, heaven's Covenant King, who reigns with purity and love.

The King Speaks through His Postexilic Prophets

Haggai encourages the people who have returned from exile to rebuild the LORD's temple. The prophet reminds them that obeying their King leads to the strength of his Spirit. God's Ruler will come and fill the rebuilt temple with glory, and the kingdoms of men will be shaken and overthrown.

Zechariah proclaims the Righteous King's rule over nations past, present, and future. The LORD "remembers" his covenant promises and acts to fulfill them. His promised return of the people from Babylonian exile and his rebuilt throne in Jerusalem's temple set the stage for a glorious future. God's Anointed King will finally and fully reclaim his rule on Earth. God's kingdom people are encouraged to return to their Loving King in spiritual renewal, and he will return to them.

Malachi affirms the Righteous King's loyal love for his restored people in the land. They had become discouraged because the glorious future announced through the Prophets hadn't been realized. Their worship had deteriorated into rituals that dishonored the LORD. Malachi calls the covenant people to take a new direction and faithfully serve their Loving King. He is coming to purify and to judge on "the day of the LORD."

Thus the Covenant King protects and enriches his loving rule in Israel through the prophets. At the same time, he builds his kingdom through the poets. As the prophets speak the King's Word, the sages speak the King's wisdom. They invite kingdom people to live meaningful and skillful lives under the reign of their Loving King.

The King Rules in Wisdom

The Poetic Books present the LORD's wise rule, and also address issues that seem to contradict his reign.

A Snapshot of the Poetic Books (Job, Psalms, Proverbs, Ecclesiastes, Song of Songs)

The Awe-Inspiring King reigns in wisdom

- **enabling his loved people to live meaningful and skillful lives in relationship with him.**

So how do the inspired poets relate to God's kingship? Here we go.

Job addresses an issue of immense significance: the just rule of Heaven's King in light of righteous people suffering. The Covenant King's reign in Israel features a simple truth: Loyal love for the LORD results in his blessing, while unfaithful disobedience results in his judgment. But that leads to the question of why righteous people suffer. That seems contradictory to God's loving reign. Why do faithful people sometimes experience not blessing, but affliction and pain?

This isn't a merely philosophical question. It is, rather, a deep and heartfelt struggle, born out of the pain of real-life experience. The issue is profound, and probes the very character of the King. Does the LORD actually rule with sovereign power and genuine love? The fact that righteous people suffer seems to contradict that idea. If the King possesses absolute power and allows the righteous to suffer, then he surely doesn't love them. If he truly loves people, and the righteous suffer, then he must not possess complete power to prevent the injustice.

Job's life story speaks to this profound issue with brilliant insight. By revealing events in heaven's courtroom before the King's throne, the author shows that there is another dimension to human experience than the simple covenant formula that faithfulness leads to blessing and unfaithfulness leads to suffering. Job makes it known that the suffering of the righteous finds its meaning in the heavenly purposes of the Awe-Inspiring King. Men may not perceive these purposes. And they must be received by faith. In the end, the Creator King's surpassing, wise reign is affirmed in both the LORD's speaking and in Job's response of humility.[112]

In addition to Job affirming the wisdom of God's rule, all of the various **Psalms** set forth the LORD as the Sovereign King who is establishing his righteous, loving rule on Earth. Enthronement Psalms joyfully proclaim "The LORD reigns!"[113] These Psalms directly celebrate the King's powerful rule and his coming to judge the rebellious world in righteousness. Royal Psalms rejoice in God's reign through the Davidic king, the LORD's representative ruler on Earth.[114] They set the human king in the foreground, yet the LORD reigns through his "son" in the holy city. Psalms of Zion delight in the King's royal residence, the site of his throne and loving reign over his people.[115] Pilgrim Psalms take joy in the journey to worship the Loving King in Jerusalem, the center of his life-giving kingdom on Earth.[116]

Certain praise Psalms exalt the King for his majestic attributes.[117] The LORD is King over all things because he created all things.[118] His powerful Word in creation sustains and governs the universe.[119] He exercises dominion over all the created order.[120] Other praise Psalms celebrate the Good King's rule in the lives of his people. Answers to prayer, victories, and deliverance from danger, death, or sin all display his loving reign on Earth.[121]

Wisdom Psalms teach insight for embracing the Righteous King's rule.[122] Several, especially Psalm 119, focus on the exceptional value of the LORD's Law. Lament Psalms cry out for the Compassionate King to demonstrate his ruling power in life situations of distress.[123] The King's response in answering the worshiper's prayer both affirms his loving rule and extends his reign on Earth.

In all of these ways, the Psalms declare that the LORD rules as the Loving, Sovereign King.

The book of **Proverbs** presents a royal collection of the King's wisdom. Inspired as jewels of crystallized spiritual truth, the LORD's wisdom is designed to enable kingdom people to live skillfully under his reign.[124] Every aspect of life is addressed. Wisdom's overarching, essential principle, as you would expect, affirms the Covenant King's rule. "The fear of the LORD is the beginning of wisdom."[125] "The fear of the LORD" brings together two components: an attitude of deep reverence for the Loving King, and a high regard for his revealed truth. A skillful life is built by awe for the Holy King, which leads to obeying his Word.[126]

Ecclesiastes conducts a firsthand investigation into the meaning of life. Qoheleth, the wise teacher, observes various pursuits "under the sun." He finds that without God, life is meaningless. The inspired sage concludes where Proverbs begins: "fear God and keep his commandments."[127] A meaningful life is lived in faithful relationship with the Loving King.

The Song of Songs celebrates one of the Good King's exquisite gifts, romantic love in the covenant of marriage. The delightful gift of sensual love in the bond of marriage echoes back to the LORD's majestic kingdom in creation.

The Wisdom Books, each in its own unique way, enrich the LORD's reign over his treasured family. Kingdom people are favored to live meaningful and skillful lives in relationship with their King.

Like all the Old Testament revelation, the prophets and poets point to King Jesus. He is the fulfillment of the prophets. He doesn't just speak God's Word; he *is* God's Living Word, the fullness of the Creator King's communication. The Word became flesh, and lived among us.[128] God spoke through the prophets, but he speaks most fully through his Son. King Jesus is the radiance of God's glory, and the exact representation of his Person.[129]

Jesus is also the fulfillment of the poets. He possesses all the rich treasures of God's wisdom.[130] King Jesus reigns with perfect skill.

Congratulations! You have now walked with the King through the entire Old Testament. That's quite a long journey. Feeling a little tired? Take heart (and maybe a rest). It all leads to the main event. The best is yet to come!

Chapter Five

The Gospels

His Loving Majesty Arrives in Person

Heaven's King doesn't speak on Earth for four hundred years after the last Old Testament Prophet, Malachi. His Word in previous kingdom history is recorded, but no fresh words are spoken. No prophet. No sage. No inspired spokesperson. That's why the four centuries leading up to the first Christmas are called "the silent years."

Why does the King of Heaven remain silent on Earth? I don't know. But speculation is that he chose a long, pregnant pause before the main event. His way of highlighting history's central act, the invasion of God's Anointed King!

Before we investigate, let's take time to review. It all leads to King Jesus.

Snapshot Review

The "Big Idea" of the Bible
God reclaims his righteous, loving rule over a rebellious world
through his Anointed King, Jesus, who

- triumphs over Satan's evil on the cross,

- rescues, in supreme love, people under the curse of sin and death,
- and fashions a magnificent New Creation under his reign,
  to the praise of his glorious grace!

Genesis 1–11
The Life-Giving King creates his majestic kingdom on Earth, but human rebellion ruins it with sin and death.

Genesis 12 through Deuteronomy
The Creator King forms Israel as his loved kingdom on Earth, in order to triumph over the curse of death and give life to all the peoples of the world.

Historical Books (Joshua through Nehemiah)
The Covenant King exercises his faithful rule during the highs and lows of Israel's history, all in anticipation of sending his Anointed King into the world.

Prophets (Isaiah through Malachi)
The Loving King guards his reign through his messengers, the prophets.

Poets (Job, Psalms, Proverbs, Ecclesiastes, Song of Songs)
The Awe–Inspiring King reigns in wisdom, enabling his people to live meaningful and skillful lives in relationship with him.

Jesus's arrival on the planet is without precedent. It is the pivotal point in human history. The LORD had exercised his loving reign on Earth for centuries in and through Israel. But Jesus of Nazareth shows God's rule in a new and profound way. He displays the very presence of the Majestic King on Earth, in bodily form. The son of Mary proves to be the son of Eve, the powerful Person God promised would crush Satan and triumph over his reign of death. The son of Abraham comes to bring life to all the peoples of the world. The Gospels capture it.

A Snapshot of the Gospels (Matthew, Mark, Luke, John)

Heaven's Anointed King, Jesus, displays God's rule with absolute power and supreme love, through

- **his supernatural birth,**
- **his life of teaching and miracles,**
- **and his death and resurrection,**
    which triumphs over Satan and the curse of sin and death
    and gives life to all people who turn to him in faith.

Why Four Gospels?

The Gospel accounts capture the brilliance of King Jesus breaking into history with God's kingdom. Have you ever wondered why there are four of them? The answer lies in the fact that each Gospel emphasizes a different aspect of Jesus's Person and work. Together, they present a richer and fuller portrait of God's Anointed King. One headline would not do full justice to His Majesty.

Matthew announces Jesus's identity as God's Anointed King, the royal Son of David, Israel's Messiah predicted by the prophets. The inspired tax collector begins with a genealogy to demonstrate the King's royal bloodline. Not every person born qualifies to be a king (few do). Jesus does. His ancestry traces back to David and Abraham.[131] You'll remember those two kingdom champions. The Creator King promises to bring life to all peoples of the world through the son of Abraham. Jesus is the One![132] Likewise, the Covenant King promises an eternal reign through the Son of David. You got it, Jesus again![133] That's why international seekers asked, "Where is the one who has been born king of the Jews? We saw his star when it rose and have come to worship him."[134] Jesus came as the prophesied Davidic King to Israel. But his rejection opens the door for all people to enter God's kingdom.[135]

Mark shines the light on the Anointed King's dynamic power. His all-powerful acts display the full authority of the Creator King. The Sovereign Servant of the LORD came not to be served, but to serve and to give his life to rescue rebels from the power of sin and death.[136] **Luke** highlights King Jesus as the Savior of the world. The non-Jewish Gospel writer traces Jesus's ancestry back through David and Abraham, to Adam.[137] Jesus extends God's life-giving reign to the entire human family of sinners.[138] **John** presents King Jesus in the full majestic splendor of his deity. Jesus is God, incarnate.[139] He is the Creator King in bodily form. God the Son came to Earth to reveal Heaven's King and to give life to all who receive him.[140] The much-loved disciple identifies Jesus as the eternal Word of God who shines light and life into the dark world of death.

Together the Gospel writers present a masterful portrait of Jesus. God's Anointed King, Sovereign Servant of the LORD, Savior of the world, life-giving Son of God. The world has never seen such an awe-inspiring king!

Absolute Power

Jesus breaks into history with God's kingdom at Christmas. What a gift! The birth of this baby in Bethlehem shows God's all-powerful reign on Earth. The King of the universe fashions a totally unique life, son of Mary, Son of the Most High.[141]

The very words "virgin birth" are a contradiction. Who can fathom a miracle of such magnitude? The Sovereign King creates a union of divinity and humanity. The Word becomes flesh, the fullness of deity in bodily form, God's Majesty in person. The Conquering King invades to recapture his rule.

So it's no surprise that Jesus kicks off his life of service with the announcement that God's kingdom has arrived.[142] Everything he says and everything he does radiates the reign of Heaven's King on Earth. He tells masterful stories about God's rule breaking into people's lives, "parables of the kingdom."[143] Unlike other professors, who rely upon recognized experts, Jesus's teaching communicates personal authority.[144] His words ring true, because he is the Truth.[145] But he doesn't just preach a good game. His works back up his words. Jesus's miracles display God's absolute power on Earth. Over everything!

In a series of video clips,[146] Mark films Jesus exercising sovereign authority over hostile forces of creation (he calms the raging sea); over destructive satanic powers (he sets free the uncontrollable demon-possessed man); and over incurable disease (he heals the woman's untreatable bleeding disorder). Then, in the ultimate display of God's life-giving power over hostile forces, he raises Jairus's daughter out of death to life. Don't miss the message: King Jesus possesses absolute power over all things, threatening physical forces, evil spiritual forces, sickness, and even death.

Jesus openly displays the kingdom of heaven on Earth. The Creator King rules perfectly in heaven. There are no dangers in heaven. No demons are permitted there. No diseases in heaven, and certainly no death. When Jesus encounters these forces on Earth, his decree instantly conquers them. He rules with the perfect, loving, and life-giving power of Heaven's King. That's why the arrival of God's kingdom on Earth is such good news![147]

Supreme Love

Along with demonstrating God's perfect power, Jesus displays his supreme love. Before Jesus, the LORD had shown his love in countless ways in creation and in his covenant with Israel. With Jesus's arrival, it would now shine forth in its fullest beauty. Every detail of Jesus's life displays love for people. He pours himself out teaching heaven's insight to crowds on Earth. He reaches out to the rejected, welcomes the outcasts, feeds the hungry, and heals the sick. The world has never seen a life so totally given over to caring for the needs of others. But his life of selfless service is the pregame warm up for his greatest act of love—the very reason he invaded the planet, the cross. The Powerful Servant's willingness to suffer the cross reveals the full dimensions of his love.[148]

Substitutionary sacrifice. King Jesus lays aside his absolute power, and filled with love, steps in to pay the death penalty for sinful rebels. The cross is where the price of justice is paid, yet where the King's love prevails. Beyond the physical horrors of death by crucifixion, Jesus suffers untold spiritual agony for the wickedness of the world.[149] He endures unfathomable pain on the cross, all to set the lawbreaker free; to grant life to all who would receive his love. His is a forgiving love, a sacrificial love, a love that is stronger than death. An incomparable love. The Conquering King's heart of love fully shown.

King Jesus's resurrection displays another measure of his power. After suffering death, he doesn't simply return to his former life before the cross. That in itself would've been a great victory. But, far more wonderful, he's transformed to a powerful new life. A glorified, resurrection body.[150] Its further proof that Jesus is heaven's Conquering King.[151]

Jesus's resurrection changes everything. When he dies on the cross, Satan strikes his heel. But when King Jesus rises from the dead, he delivers the evil one a skull-crushing deathblow.[152] He destroys the devil's work.[153] He disarms his power of death.[154] And, in supreme love, he sets free prisoners who were held captive in the serpent's domain of death.[155]

King Jesus's victory is complete. Perfect! It's death-destroying and life-giving. Guilty rebels who turn to him in faith are released from Satan's dungeon of death and enter Jesus's kingdom of life and love. Our astonishing destiny is now Jesus's victory of a glorified resurrection life,[156] reigning with him in his New Creation.

Kingdom Fullness and Future

Jesus is both the fullness of God's kingdom and the future of God's kingdom. He fulfills every dimension of the LORD's reign in Israel. The full picture would take volumes, so we'll stick with Bible Cliff Notes.

Jesus is the son of Eve who crushes Satan.[157] His death and resurrection triumph over the curse of sin and death.[158] He fulfills the LORD's promise to Abraham of granting life to all peoples of the world.[159] He fulfills the Passover,[160] the blood of the sacrificial Lamb shed to deliver us from death into a relationship with the Rescuing King. He lives out the righteousness of the Law.[161]

Every shadow of the Tabernacle finds its true image in King Jesus:

- the altar (sacrifice)[162]
- the laver (cleansing)[163]
- the bread of Presence (nourishment and relationship)[164]
- the lampstand (illumination)[165]
- the golden altar of incense (prayer)[166]
- the torn veil (access)[167]
- the mercy seat (atonement)[168]

He fulfills the Levitical offerings:

- the whole burnt offering (surrender and acceptance)[169]
- the grain offering (devoted labor)[170]
- the fellowship offering (peace, well-being)[171]
- the sin offering (atonement)[172]
- the reparation offering (compensation for damages)[173]

He is the substance of the kingdom's worship festivals:[174]

- Passover (rescue)
- Unleavened Bread (purity)
- First Fruits (resurrection)
- Pentecost (Church age)
- Trumpets (Rapture)

- Day of Atonement (Second Coming)
- Tabernacles (New Creation)

Jesus completes and perfects the three anointed offices in Israel's kingdom. He is the ultimate prophet, the fullest revelation of God.[175] He is the true high priest, serving between God and his people.[176] He is the quintessential King, fulfilling the LORD's promise to David of an eternal dynasty.[177]

He initiates the New Covenant,[178] embodies the LORD's wisdom,[179] fulfills and will fulfill the visions of the prophets.

That pretty much covers the Old Testament revelation, doesn't it? King Jesus achieves the full dimensions of God's reign on Earth. He also is the future of God's kingdom. Jesus, himself, declares the present–future dynamic of God's rule. On the one hand, he affirms that God's kingdom is presently active in history. He says, "Truly I tell you, the tax collectors and the prostitutes are entering the kingdom of God ahead of you."[180] On another occasion he says, "But if I drive out demons by the finger of God, then the kingdom of God has come upon you."[181] Jesus's powerful acts show that God's reign is presently active on Earth.

On the other hand, King Jesus declares that the fullness of his rule will take place in the future. The perfect realization of his kingdom awaits his Second Coming.

> When the Son of Man comes in his glory, and all the angels with him, he will sit on his glorious throne. All the nations will be gathered before him, and he will separate the people one from another as a shepherd separates the sheep from the goats. He will put the sheep on his right and the goats on his left. Then the King will say to those on his right, "Come, you who are blessed by my Father; take your inheritance, the kingdom prepared for you since the creation of the world." [182]

Jesus further speaks of the future fulfillment of his kingdom when he gives instruction for communion. At his last supper with the disciples, the night before he is crucified, he tells his followers to regularly remember his loving sacrifice on the cross. He gives them the bread and the cup that represent his body and blood. Then he says, "Truly I tell you, I will not drink again from the fruit of the vine until that day when I drink it new in the kingdom of God."[183]

In light of his future appearance, the Lord Jesus urges his family to prepare for history's climactic event. Matthew records a string of the King's perceptive parables that are designed to help us strike a balance in kingdom living while we anticipate his return to Earth.[184]

Jesus's story of the homeowner and thief warns us to keep an alert watch. The Returning King will come when he's *not expected*. The parable of the absent master inspires us to serve faithfully. The Son of Man may come *sooner than expected*. The video of the ten bridesmaids prompts us to plan wisely. The Bridegroom King may come *later than expected*. The parable of the talents urges us to invest diligently the resources that the King has given us to manage. He is coming *to inspect* our investments. He will hold people accountable, with both rewards and judgment. The story of the sheep and goats reveals that the Just King will come in heavenly glory *to judge* the nations. He will separate people into one of two destinies: eternal life in the kingdom of God, or eternal judgment. The determining factor is a living faith expressed in kingdom works. Together, the King's parables provide wise insight so we can live ready for God's future kingdom, coming to your neighborhood when the King returns.

In every way, King Jesus displays God's perfect reign on Earth. Absolute power. Supreme love. Present reality. Future realization. God's kingdom has come! Yes, but not fully. Get ready for the Church. It's the hope of the world.

Chapter Six

Acts and New Testament Letters

The Risen King Launches a New Kingdom People, the Church

The Gospels capture King Jesus breaking into history with absolute power and supreme love. After he conquers the power of death and ascends to the highest place in heaven, you might think his work on Earth is done. But in some ways, it's just beginning. The Risen King sends the Holy Spirit and launches a new movement, the Church. The Church is a new community of people who receive his reign. No longer made up of members of just one nation, Israel, this new community embraces people from every nation. The Church is a new family, in a New Covenant, with a new mission. It's the dawn of a new day in God's rule on Earth! God initiates a new kingdom people, the Church.

Before we explore this new kingdom movement, time to review. "Repetition is the mother of all learning," a wise mentor once told me (yes, it was my mother). Can you think your way through the major kingdom movements?

Snapshot Review

The "Big Idea" of the Bible
God reclaims his righteous, loving rule over a rebellious world
    through his Anointed King, Jesus, who

- triumphs over Satan's evil on the cross,
- rescues, in supreme love, people under the curse of sin and death,
- and fashions a magnificent New Creation under his reign,
    to the praise of his glorious grace!

Genesis 1–11
The Life-Giving King creates his majestic kingdom on Earth, but human rebellion ruins it with sin and death.

Genesis 12 through Deuteronomy
The Creator King forms Israel as his loved kingdom on Earth, in order to triumph over the curse of death and give life to all the peoples of the world.

Historical Books (Joshua through Nehemiah)
The Covenant King exercises his faithful rule during the highs and lows of Israel's history, all in anticipation of sending his Anointed King into the world.

Prophets (Isaiah through Malachi)
The Loving King guards his reign through his messengers, the prophets.

Poets (Job, Psalms, Proverbs, Ecclesiastes, Song of Songs)
The Awe–Inspiring King reigns in wisdom, enabling his people to live meaningful and skillful lives in relationship with him.

The Gospels (Matthew, Mark, Luke, John)
King Jesus displays God's rule with absolute power and supreme love.

Now let's look at the next development in God's kingdom.

A Snapshot of Acts and the New Testament Letters

The Risen King, Jesus, launches a new kingdom on Earth of Spirit-empowered believers, to

- **represent his loving presence in the world,**
- **and advance his life–giving reign among the nations,**
  until he returns to recreate all things under his righteous rule.

An Unexpected New Kingdom People

The Church's birth in history is a surprise.[185] No one saw it coming. The Prophets of Israel had foreseen the LORD's reign of spiritual blessing extending to non-Jewish peoples. But the Covenant King kept it a big secret that he was going to adopt a new family. His new family on Earth would be Jewish and Gentile believers knit together as brothers and sisters, fellow members of Christ's kingdom and joint heirs of the Conquering King. It was all an unexpected variation in God's rule on Earth. The truth is, angels on high marvel at the brilliant crown jewel of the King's wisdom, the Church![186] (And you thought it was just a place to hang out for coffee and donuts on Sunday morning. Hopefully not.)

King Jesus's launch of the Church creates new dimensions for God's kingdom. He initiates profound changes in God's reign on Earth. Israel had been a defined nation, a particular ethnic group living in a specific territory with geographical borders. The nation was ruled by a prescribed human government under the LORD's kingship. God's kingdom now includes people from every race and ethnic background. It rises beyond territorial borders to include people from every nation on the planet. And one Mediator King governs it worldwide.[187] (Despite what you may have been taught, your church pastor is not the human king, unfortunately, says this pastor.)

A New Kingdom Relationship

Members of the new kingdom relate to the LORD not through the covenant made at Sinai, but through a New Covenant, one set forth by the Conquering King at the cross.[188] Believers now receive forgiveness and a relationship with the King through his victory over the curse of sin and death. The New Covenant King fulfills the righteousness of the Law,[189] nails the Law to the cross,[190] and removes it from his reign over the Church.[191] The LORD still desires righteous people. So in the New Covenant, he writes his righteous law on our hearts. He governs our lives through the indwelling Holy Spirit.[192]

A New Kingdom Power

That's another seismic shift in God's reign on Earth. In Israel's covenant, the Holy Spirit was given to select individuals to empower them for their particular kingdom service. He also was given conditionally to people, and could vacate the premises, if you will, by leaving a person.[193] In the New Covenant, the Holy Spirit is granted to every believer. That's the beauty of Pentecost. He is the birthright of every Christian,[194] and he is a permanent resident. We are sealed by the Holy Spirit.[195] That means we're marked as belonging to King Jesus and we are secured in our relationship with him.

So the Church era of God's rule on Earth could well be called the Spirit era. The Generous King's gift of the Holy Spirit strengthens his family members in a number of ways. The Holy Spirit gives us assurance of salvation.[196] He teaches,[197] guides,[198] and prays for us.[199] He sets us free from the control of sin,[200] enables our spiritual growth,[201] and gives us courage to tell people about Jesus.[202] He pours out the King's love in our hearts and strengthens us to love others.[203] He gives us spiritual gifts for service.[204] He nurtures the King's beauty in our lives: love, joy, peace, patience, kindness, goodness, faithfulness, gentleness, and self-control.[205] He assures us of our identity as fellow heirs of God's Anointed King.[206]

Did you catch that last one? We receive an inheritance that makes the combined net worth of Earth's billionaires look like chump change. Our inheritance is an eternal treasure that is beyond our capacity to imagine. "No eye has seen, no ear has heard, and no mind has imagined what God has prepared for those who love him."[207]

In every way, King Jesus has richly resourced us with the gift of the Holy Spirit. Both for our present life, and also for the world to come. We live in the bountiful Age of the Spirit.

A New Kingdom Mission

Having triumphed over the curse of sin and death on the cross, the Risen King Jesus gives new marching orders to those who receive his reign.[208] Our mission?

- to announce the good news of his profound love and victory on the cross
- to relay his offer of life to all who receive him
- to baptize believers into their new life
- to nurture their growth in King Jesus's reign by teaching them to obey his Word
- to participate in the Holy Spirit's work of drawing new members into the Lord's forever family[209]
- in summary, to increase Jesus's reign among the nations

King Jesus delegates his new mission not to a bunch of individuals, but to a new community. The hope of the world[210] is released through his new family.[211] Ever since the LORD intercepted Abraham, and through his covenant with Israel, he has shown himself to be the Family King. Relationships are central and vital to his mission on Earth. So he forms a new community for his new mission, the Church. One kingdom people, comprised of local church families in every country on the planet. All serving to extend his reign on Earth.

An Organic Connection

In carrying out our mission to advance God's kingdom on Earth, two elements of King Jesus's new reign are vitally important. First, Heaven's King is vitally bonded with us in a living unity. The nature of the relationship is spiritually organic—whatever that means! Here's the image: He is the head, and we are the body. We are indivisibly united with him in a living relationship. Just think about the kind of living unity that this image conveys. Either the head without the body, or the body without the head, would be an ugly atrocity. The head and the body are vital parts of one another. The relationship is so joined together that the believer is identified as "in God's Anointed King" (that is, "in Christ").[212] We experience "Christ in us," [213] through the indwelling presence of the King's Holy Spirit.

The importance of this living unity can't be overemphasized. It's vital to the Lord's life-giving mission. King Jesus uses another organic image to communicate our relationship with him: He is the Vine, and we are the branches.[214] Only if we are vitally connected to him will his life flow into us, giving life to all sorts of good gifts in us, and in his reign on Earth.

Unity with Diversity

The head–body image of King Jesus's unity with us conveys another profound truth concerning our relationships within the church family. We are individual members of one body. Each member is unique, and each member is necessary and valuable for the healthy functioning of the body. All parts need one another to be complete. The variety of parts, by design, includes more than individual differences in God-given personality, talents, or backgrounds. The diversity embraces the life of the Spirit, since each of us receives a unique combination of spiritual gifts.[215]

Our relationships in the body of Christ involve unity; we are one body. They involve a rich diversity; each member is uniquely gifted. And they are designed to produce growth to maturity.[216] The whole body, and each individual member, grows into the fullness of Christ, as each member serves with his or her spiritual gifts. Service is inspired by love for King Jesus, and love for one another. The entire process shows the Lord Jesus's reign, in and through the church. And it is vital to his mission on Earth.

King Jesus's Love is Released

That leads us to the second essential element of King Jesus's relationship with his new kingdom people. Having displayed his supreme heart of love on the cross, Jesus now releases his love on Earth through his family. He desires for his powerful love, poured into our hearts, to overflow to others.[217]

Once again, this element of the King's reign can't be overstated. Our love for people is vitally connected with our primary purpose in life, loving God.[218] Loving others is also essential for showing his rule to the nations. As Jesus puts it, "By this will all people know that you are my followers, that you love one another."[219] People must know that God's Anointed King is love, in personal form. The truth is, if the King's genuine love is not alive in us, our service is all pretty much worthless—no, totally worthless. Without his love energizing us, our lives are useless, like a clanging gong.[220]

Love matters. We must genuinely represent Heaven's King on Earth. We are his personal presence on the planet—his feet, his hands, and his caring heart. His love with skin on.

New Kingdom Communication

The Risen King reveals his reign to his new kingdom family through the apostles and prophets.[221] New messengers write the New Testament books. Here is a tweet of their messages.

Acts records the Conquering King's launch of his new community on Earth. The Lord Jesus births the Church by pouring out the Holy Spirit on believers in Jerusalem. He thus empowers his new family to represent him on Earth and to advance his reign among the nations. Dr. Luke films the Church's birth on the Day of Pentecost, as well as its early years of development from Jerusalem to Rome. His footage includes the kingdom's growth to become a blended family, embracing Jewish and Gentile members in one body.

Romans presents a well-organized explanation of the King's good news, the basis for entering his kingdom. The righteousness God requires from all sin-cursed people is granted by his generous grace, and it's received by faith in the Lord Jesus. Through such faith, God's Anointed King sets his family members free. Totally free! Believers are free from the penalty for their sinful rebellion (death). They are also free from the power of sin to rule their lives. The Loving King enables his people to live righteous lives through the power of the indwelling Holy Spirit. Having received such favor, rescued rebels are urged to give themselves fully to loving their King.

1 Corinthians instructs the New Covenant community about King Jesus's reign in their congregation. The Apostle Paul addresses practical issues such as unity, righteousness, marriage, and worship practices, including the exercise of spiritual gifts, the preeminence of love, and resurrection. Along with the other New Testament books, this letter shows that Jesus's reign over his family is not automatic. It must be learned and lived. In **2 Corinthians**, Paul champions God's kingdom by defending King Jesus's authority that was assigned to him, the Lord's appointed messenger, against the challenges made by false teachers. He also instructs believers concerning the true nature and high calling of serving their King as agents of the New Covenant, and encourages generosity.

Galatians refutes false teaching, which threatens to jeopardize King Jesus's reign on Earth by distorting his good news. Kingdom people become righteous by faith alone in the Lord Jesus, apart from works of the Law. This means they are free to live a New Covenant life in the power of the Holy Spirit. The former requirements of Israel's covenant must not be imposed on the new kingdom family. **Ephesians** celebrates the invasion of the Conquering King's grace, with his lavish provision of spiritual benefits for his people. Each Person of the triune God is praised for the blessings he gives, which flow from the LORD's rich generosity and undeserved favor. The new kingdom community of the Church is declared. Created as a masterpiece of grace and peace, the church family must honor King Jesus by living out their new identities in their new lifestyle on Earth.

Philippians encourages God's kingdom people to live lives worthy of heaven's Servant King, and to live joyfully in every circumstance. The Apostle Paul thanks the church family for their generosity, an admirable reflection of their King, and warns them about false teachers. **Colossians** declares the absolute sufficiency of the Lord Jesus. He reigns supreme over the universe and the Church. His authoritative truth must, therefore, be received. And the emptiness of human philosophy, which seeks to slither into the church, must be rejected. The King is guarding against false teaching that threatens to corrupt his reign.

1 and 2 Thessalonians encourage the church family to live in a manner that honors their Returning King. He will arrive at any moment to claim his people and reclaim his perfect rule on Earth.

1 Timothy builds God's new community on his truth (sound doctrine). The Conquering King guards his kingdom from Satan's forces of darkness, namely, false teachers and deceiving spirits who seek to ruin his realm on Earth. The inspired apostle further instructs the church in practical matters of faith and life under Jesus's loving rule. **2 Timothy** urges servants of King Jesus to faithful courage in the face of hardship.

Titus further instructs the Loving King's community in matters of life and sound doctrine. **Philemon** urges kingdom people to show the Lord's grace to one another in all the circumstances of their lives. **Hebrews** declares the absolute supremacy of King Jesus over God's former rule in the form of Israel's covenant, which has been fulfilled and replaced. New Covenant believers are urged to press on serving their Preeminent King-Priest amid the persecution they suffer.

James urges kingdom citizens to a living faith in God's Anointed King, emphasizing that this produces vital works. **1 Peter** encourages God's new community of treasured people to live distinctive lives when suffering persecution, in the wake of their rejected Holy King. **2 Peter** spurs God's New Covenant family to pursue spiritual growth. King Jesus guards again against false teachers who seek to infiltrate the church. He is returning in judgment to reign over his New Creation.

1 John strengthens kingdom people in their faith by countering false teachings about King Jesus, and by affirming the basis on which believers are assured of their relationship with him. **2 and 3 John** instruct God's family to exercise discernment before supporting traveling teachers. False messengers oppose God's kingdom. Yet believers are commended for helping true servants of the King who advance his reign. **Jude** calls believers to hold on to the truth about God's saving grace, against false teachers who pervert it and who will face the Just King's judgment.

Through the New Testament writings, King Jesus instructs, protects, and encourages his New Covenant family to pursue kingdom living. A consistent theme runs through these inspired books. The Risen and Reigning King is returning, at any moment, to fully reclaim his rule on Earth and to recreate the universe. So it's urgent to embrace his kingship now. The day is dawning for history's Grand Finale!

Chapter Seven

Revelation

The Grand Finale! King Jesus Returns to Fully Reclaim God's Majestic Rule over a New Creation

At his first arrival in history, God's Anointed King came in humility, to serve and to suffer. He was born in an animal shelter, in the form of a servant. Only a few people—some lowly sheepherders and foreign nobles—witnessed the event. His mission was to triumph over the curse of sin through his death on the cross. At his second arrival, King Jesus will come riding on the clouds of heaven. His absolute majesty will be on full display. Every person on the planet will see the King's supreme glory and power. His mission will be to exercise judgment and to finally reestablish his rightful rule.

The day of the LORD will be a dreadful day for a rebellious world. God's Anointed King will unleash a devastating judgment, the likes of which has never been seen before. The cancer of evil on planet Earth will be totally destroyed. The Conquering King will purge the Earth. He will rebirth the universe and set creation free from its bondage to death. He will fully reclaim his righteous rule by reigning over a glorified New Creation. There he will display the fullness of his loving, life-giving presence—the fullness of his majestic Person. An absolutely glorious finale!

The final book of the Bible presents the climactic events of God's rule breaking in on Earth. We will add this last snapshot to our kingdom album. But first, one more review of the big picture. Then there will be a written final exam, which you must pass in order to enter God's kingdom (just kidding).

Snapshot Review

The "Big Idea" of the Bible

God reclaims his righteous, loving rule over a rebellious world
  through his Anointed King, Jesus, who

- triumphs over Satan's evil on the cross,
- rescues, in supreme love, people under the curse of sin and death,
- and fashions a magnificent New Creation under his reign,
    to the praise of his glorious grace!

Genesis 1–11

The Life–Giving King creates his majestic kingdom on Earth, but human rebellion ruins it with sin and death.

Genesis 12 through Deuteronomy

The Creator King forms Israel as his loved kingdom on Earth, in order to triumph over the curse of death and give life to all the peoples of the world.

Historical Books (Joshua through Nehemiah)

The Covenant King exercises his faithful rule during the highs and lows of Israel's history, all in anticipation of sending his Anointed King into the world.

Prophets (Isaiah through Malachi)

The Loving King guards his reign through his messengers, the prophets.

Poets (Job, Psalms, Proverbs, Ecclesiastes, Song of Songs)
The Awe–Inspiring King reigns in wisdom, enabling his people to live meaningful and skillful lives in relationship with him.

The Gospels (Matthew, Mark, Luke, John)
King Jesus displays God's rule with absolute power and supreme love.

Acts and New Testament Letters (Romans through Jude)
The Risen King, Jesus, launches a new kingdom people, the Church.

A Snapshot of Revelation

The Conquering King, Jesus, exercises his righteous, life–giving rule over a rebellious planet, by

- **reigning over the Church,**
- **unleashing future, catastrophic judgment on a rebellious world,**
- **and returning in majesty to reign in love over his New Creation.**

The book of Revelation is, in many ways, a strange and confusing book. It's filled with visions, some puzzling symbols, and weird images. But don't miss the truth of the book's title, "The Revelation of Jesus Christ." It's a volume written to reveal the identity of God's Anointed King. The book proclaims three vital truths about King Jesus: He is the glorious Ruler of the Church.[222] He is the worthy Judge of the world.[223] And he is the life-giving King of the New Creation.[224] King Jesus exercises God's perfect rule, both now and forever!

King-Priest Reigning over the Church

In the first three chapters of Revelation, the Apostle John receives a vision of Jesus. He is heaven's majestic King-Priest,[225] the Glorious One among the churches. He exercises his reign over congregations on Earth in a number of ways.[226] He commends loyalty and faith amid persecution. He rebukes those who disregard his love, and those who practice idolatry, immorality, and indifference. He patiently calls people to repent and fully embrace his loving rule in every area of their lives. He strengthens his persecuted family with promises of eternal life. He encourages them with his desire to grant them honor. He inspires his loved sons and daughters with the vision of sharing in his reign over the New Creation.

King Jesus shows his credentials to reign over the Church when he shares his personal testimony with John, "I am the First and the Last. I am the Living One; I was dead, and now look, I am alive for ever and ever! And I hold the keys of death and Hades."[227] Jesus rules with absolute power because he is eternal, victorious over death, and possesses authority over the world to come.

Worthy Judge of the World

King Jesus reigns over the Church from heaven now. Yet the day is coming when he will exercise his rule as worthy Judge on Earth.[228] The inspired Apostle is lifted in a vision into the resplendent throne room of heaven.[229] The angelic realm is worshiping the King of the universe. A strong angel challenges the entire creation to identify a candidate worthy to judge the Earth. Tragically, no one qualifies. John is troubled to tears. Satan's throne on the planet[230] will go unchallenged, his evil reign unchecked.

But hope is on the horizon. A sudden announcement rings forth. A worthy candidate is presented! It's a powerful King, the Lion of the tribe of Judah, the Root of David. King Jesus is qualified to judge and to reign. He has conquered death and he possesses absolute authority[231] and complete knowledge.[232] He sees all things and has perfect power to execute justice. So he is uniquely able to judge the world.

The powerful Lion of the tribe of Judah will roar in judgment on Earth. But he is also the Lamb of God. The Savior who gave his life, in supreme love, to rescue rebels from every nation and make them heirs of his eternal reign.[233] He is absolutely worthy of praise! John's weeping, at that point, is overwhelmed by worship. Praise bursts forth throughout the universe, creatures on Earth and angels in heaven rejoicing together.

The Apostle then receives a vision of that dreadful day foreseen by the prophets and apostles: The day of the LORD.[234] The four horsemen of the Apocalypse—Conquest, War, Famine, Death—ride forth. From seals to trumpets to bowls of wrath, the judgment intensifies. The kingdom of God is coming to Earth, with increasing devastation. The Conquering King pours out his righteous wrath on a rebellious planet. Heaven testifies that his judgments are just. The song of the righteous declares,

> Great and marvelous are your deeds, Lord God Almighty. Just and true are your ways, King of the nations. Who will not fear you, Lord, and bring glory to your name? For you alone are holy. All nations will come and worship before you, for your righteous acts have been revealed.[235]

> You are just in these judgments, O Holy One…Yes, Lord God Almighty, true and just are your judgments.[236]

The Just King's catastrophic judgments prompt two responses on Earth. On one hand, countless numbers of people from every nation receive the merciful Lamb's rule. They sing, "Salvation belongs to our God, who sits on the throne, and to the Lamb."[237] On the other hand, despite the intensifying disasters, rebels harden their hearts and refuse to turn to the Good King's grace. They persist in their wickedness and evil acts.

> The rest of mankind who were not killed by these plagues still did not repent of the work of their hands; they did not stop worshiping demons, and idols of gold, silver, bronze, stone and wood—idols that cannot see or hear or walk. Nor did they repent of their murders, their magic arts, their sexual immorality or their thefts.[238]

[T]hey cursed the name of God, who had control over these plagues, but they refused to repent and glorify him…[people] cursed the God of heaven because of their pains and their sores, but they refused to repent of what they had done.[239]

The Conquering King's dreadful judgment reaches a climax with the destruction of "Babylon the Great." [240] The rebellious empire of detestable practices on Earth, ruled by Satan and his vile forces, is crushed. All heaven celebrates and praises God![241] The radiant Light finally destroys the devil's domain of darkness. King Jesus defeats and eliminates the reign of evil on Earth. The Righteous, Loving King prevails.

Returning in Glory to Rule

Heaven's rejoicing anticipates the awesome arrival on Earth of God's Anointed King.[242] He rides triumphantly on a white horse. The hosts of heaven ride in procession, also on white horses, and wearing white linen. He is the Victorious Judge. The Quintessential King!

King Jesus's character is on full display. He is Faithful and True. He sees with penetrating and holy discernment. His eyes, "like blazing fire," radiate justice. He possesses all power. "Out of his mouth comes a sharp sword with which to strike down the nations." He is the LORD's supreme revelation. His "Name is the Word of God." He possesses absolute authority to rule. "On his head are many crowns." "On his robe and on his thigh he has this name written: 'KING OF KINGS AND LORD OF LORDS.'" He is magnificent in mystery, beyond comprehension. He has a "name written on him that no one knows but himself."

Heaven's Anointed King wages holy war on Earth. He destroys his wicked enemies and resurrects faithful family members to reign with him. He exercises final judgment at his Great White Throne.[243] Satan, the deceiver of Eve and the nations, is cast into eternal judgment, along with those who stand in defiance with him. The evil rebellion is finally and ultimately crushed. The cancer of sin on Earth is completely eliminated. Death itself is terminated. The planet is purged for the new world to come.

Life-Giving King of the New Creation

The Bible's last scene pictures the spectacular majesty of the New Heaven and the New Earth.[244] The Conquering King fully reclaims his majestic reign over a rebellious world. He recreates the universe, making it even more magnificent than his original masterpiece.

At the center of the New Creation is the King's holy city, the New Jerusalem. The celestial city shines with resplendent brilliance, the very glory of God. Its construction displays supreme splendor—perfect symmetry, colossal magnitude, and spectacular beauty, like nothing the world has ever seen. The Architect King's most glorious palace!

The true magnificence of the city, though, is found in its Resident Royalty. God the Father and his Anointed King, Jesus, reign from their thrones in the holy city. The New Kingdom is marked by glory and honor. The curse of sin and death, and the suffering that attends it, are all banished.

What will it be like for you and me to live in the New Creation? It will mean perfect intimacy with the Loving King. We will know fully his presence and eternal affection. We "will see his face." We will experience transformed character, the perfect excellence of King Jesus, himself. "His name will be on (our) foreheads." We will enjoy adventurous, rewarding service in the New Creation. "(We) will reign for ever and ever." We will know fullness of life. The "river of the water of life" flows from King Jesus's throne. "The tree of life" stands on each bank with a continual harvest of fruit. We will be constantly filled with life-giving joy. The sum total, eternal life, knowing the Loving Father and his Son, King Jesus, intimately.[245]

The Conquering King's absolute victory inspires all of heaven to rejoice.

> **The seventh angel trumpeted.**
> **A crescendo of voices in heaven sang out,**
> **"The kingdom of the world is now the kingdom of our God**
> **and his Anointed King!**
> **He will rule forever and ever!"**[246]

The Conquering King concludes his self-revelation with an invitation. He is the glorious Ruler of the Church, the worthy Judge of the world, and the life-giving King of the New Creation. His invitation, to all of us, is to receive life.

> The Spirit and the bride say, "Come!" And let the one who hears say, "Come!" Let the one who is thirsty come; and let the one who wishes take the free gift of the water of life.[247]

You can receive the living water today. Its fullness will flow in the New Creation, but the Loving King makes new life available now to everyone who comes to him.

Conclusion

Keys for Living in God's Kingdom Today

What is the grand narrative of the Bible? God reclaims his righteous, loving rule over a rebellious world, through his Anointed King. In supreme love, Jesus suffers death on the cross in order to triumph over Satan, conquer the curse of sin and death, and give life to all people who turn to him in faith. He returns to purge the world of evil and fashion a New Creation, more magnificent than the first. It's not paradise regained, but paradise recreated on a superior level. A greater display of his glory. A brilliant manifestation of his grace.

Seven Keys for Living in God's Kingdom Today

King Jesus's absolute majesty and coming reign on Earth raises an urgent question. How should we live now in anticipation of his awesome arrival? The Good King's Word is filled with practical insight for kingdom living in the twenty-first century. But let me focus on the one essential response, and point you to some strategic ways to make it happen.

How should wise kingdom people live today? His Majesty, himself, nails it: "Seek, first, God's kingdom."[248] Make the reign of King Jesus your personal priority. Embrace his rule over every territory of your life. That is the principle. Here are seven key ways to make it real. If you have been traveling *40 Days of God's Kingdom* in a small group (and I hope you have, because Jesus designed you to experience his kingdom in relationships), these keys serve as a review from your Study Guide. How are you doing in actually putting them into practice? Are you enthroning King Jesus over the landscape of your life, now, in preparation for his eternal rule in the New Creation?

Here are seven strategic ways to engage Jesus's reign in your life, and invite his favor.

Kingdom Key #1: Receive Jesus as your Savior King. I suspect that your interest in reading this book indicates you have already placed your faith in Jesus. But rather than make that assumption, let me ask you life's most essential and eternal question: Have you received Jesus as your Savior King? If not, this could be the best day of your life, if you turn to him in faith. It's as easy as **A, B, C.**

Admit your need.[249] Come to grips with the fact that you were born into rebellion against God, and that you have participated personally in the rebellion. Confess your disobedience to the Lord, which has grieved his loving heart. Realize that you're in desperate need of forgiveness for your sins. Without that, you remain under the just judgment of the Holy King.

Believe in Jesus.[250] Take God at his Word. Trust that Jesus's death on the cross pays the penalty for your rebellion. Trust that because he loves you, King Jesus offered himself as the just sacrifice for your sins. Trust that he sets you free from the penalty for your sins, declares you righteous, adopts you as his deeply loved son or daughter, and gives you the gift of eternal life. Receive Jesus as your Savior King by placing your trust in him.

Commit to following Jesus. Realize that his desire is to walk with you through life, and decide to pursue activities that will develop your relationship with your Loving King. The kingdom keys listed below will get you going.

If you have just made the decision to receive Jesus, congratulations! Welcome to the kingdom of God. This is the best decision you will ever make! All of heaven is rejoicing, and you have just received the buried treasure whose value no one can fully fathom. But you can start now to experience its richness.

If you have previously received Jesus as your Savior King, may I urge you to reaffirm your decision to enthrone him over every area of your life. We all have a tendency to divide our lives into various territories, and then to receive Jesus's reign over certain regions and yet reject his rule over others. We could call this selective obedience, or, perhaps more accurately, designated rebellion. In either case, it isn't a response worthy of our Loving King, and it will restrict his favor in your life. Wherever you are in your relationship with him, decide today to engage King Jesus's reign over every part of your life. Before you even read the kingdom keys below, resolve to obey them. Like Abraham, commit to following King Jesus ahead of time.

He is King of the universe. He reigns in love, and he is coming to rule over his magnificent New Creation. Prepare for his arrival, now, by bowing your knee to His Majesty. The remaining kingdom keys will make his reign real in your life.

Kingdom Key #2: Give King Jesus first place in your day. Here is a truth that boggles the mind. King Jesus created you to love you. He has gone to enormous lengths to break into history, ultimately triumphing through the cross, just so he could love you forever. He desires, above all else, to enjoy a relationship with you. Have you been captured by this overwhelming love? If so, you'll realize that your greatest response would be to love him back with all your heart.

A primary way to live this out is to devote the best time of your day to a heart-to-heart encounter with your Loving King. Simply set aside a period of time in your day to meet, alone, with him. Hear him speak to you through his Word and his Spirit. Share your heart with him in prayer. Call it your Quiet Time, Devotional Time, whatever. It's the best way to honor your King, because it gives him what he desires most, your heart.

The Lord Jesus is worthy of your best in all things, so give him the best time of your day. If you're a morning person, rise to meet with him. If you're at your best in the evening, meet with him then. The point is, give him the first and best of your heart, daily.

If meeting personally with your King is a new venture for you, Appendix 1 is a good resource that can coach you in this vital encounter. Let me give you a heads up. Consistently meeting with King Jesus will be a major battle for you. It is for all kingdom people. The reason? It's so vital for your spiritual life that the enemy will marshal everything he can in the world and in your rebellious nature to cancel these meetings. But you can prevail, through the power of your Conquering King's indwelling Spirit.

<hr />

Kingdom Key #3: Give King Jesus first place by loving people. From kingdom start to finish, relationships are vital to the Covenant King. He created them, and he desires to fill your relationships with life. What, specifically, does that mean? He wants you to have wonderful experiences at the core of your being, love, joy, peace, patience, kindness, goodness, faithfulness, gentleness, and self-control.[251] These are treasures that create rich and rewarding bonds with the people in your life.

The way to receive King Jesus's reign in your relationships, and the favor that comes with it, is through the obedience of faith. Trust him, and obey him. The Lord's command for our relationships releases inner springs of life. "Love one another. As I have loved you, so you must love one another."[252] Jesus desires that his powerful love, poured into our hearts, overflow to the people in our lives.

The King's decree to love governs all of our relationships, but especially those at the core of our lives, our family. A husband displays the Lord Jesus's reign by loving his wife with a self-giving love. He

- makes her his second priority in life, under only King Jesus himself;
- makes personal sacrifices to care for her;
- and grants her honor with his words and his actions.

A wife shows Jesus's reign by loving her husband with a self-giving love. She

- makes him her second priority under heaven's High King;
- places his need above her own;
- and shows him respect with her words and her actions.[253]

Jesus's reign shines through family members who honor their parents, who find specific ways to show their mothers and fathers they are valued and loved.[254] Parents radiate God's kingdom by teaching their children about the Lord Jesus.[255] And even more powerful than instruction, by showing them with their lives an authentic love for their King.[256]

Single people demonstrate Jesus's reign by devoting themselves to sexual purity, now, in preparation for their future spouse.[257] They embody the loyal love birthed in the heart of their King. They trust their Good Shepherd to lead them and provide their marriage partner.

The instructions for embracing Jesus's reign in our relationships are certainly challenging. But throughout kingdom history, obeying the Lord's loving commands is the way to love him, to display his kingship, and to receive his favor in our family.

Now you may be thinking, "Yeah, right! You have no idea about my family problems." True, but I do know this. King Jesus is a master at miracles. He specializes in making messes into masterpieces. When it comes to the particular challenges of your relationships, be encouraged that he will work a miracle, first, in you. Then watch for the miracle in your family. Your Generous King has given you his indwelling Spirit, your Partner in love. So as you choose to obey, rely on him during your specific circumstances to come alongside and help you. He will give you strength, grace, humility, wisdom, patience, and forgiveness. He will give you everything you need to inject life in you, and through you to your relationships.

King Jesus is honored when we love all people, those close to us as well as those who may be against us. He calls us to love our enemies.[258] The Loving King's heart, in us, is particularly tested when we interact with people who stand opposed to us, or who may hurt us. Remember that love is a choice to act in the best interests of another person, regardless of what that person's response may be. That's how King Jesus showed his love toward us. He acted in compassion and went to the cross for us, even when we stood as enemies against him, acting out of the rebellion of our sin.[259] So when we seek to love difficult people, it doesn't mean we'll have warm and wonderful feelings for them. And we certainly can't control their words or actions. But we can make a willful decision to act for their benefit. In that way, we show Christ's love.

God's kingdom also shows up on Earth when we care for the poor, the outcast, and the oppressed. A defining feature of the King's heart of love is reaching out in practical ways to help those in need.

Kingdom Key #4: Give King Jesus first place with your body. When the Creator King invaded history to create Israel as his kingdom, he chose to reside above the ark of the covenant in Jerusalem. He set his throne room—where he reigned on Earth—in Israel's temple. Amazingly, in his New Covenant rule, he situates his royal residence in a surprising place: your body.[260]

The impact of this truth is significant, to say the least! Our Loving King has placed his personal presence (his throne) in our bodies. Our body is the temple of the Holy Spirit. So we must honor His Majesty in our bodily existence. When we do, we invite his favorable reign over our physical lives.

How do we give King Jesus first place with our bodies? First, we must pursue sexual purity in our thoughts and our actions.[261] When we live in sexual purity, we embody the King's presence, and we experience the joys of healthy and rewarding relationships, whether we're single or married.

A second very practical way we enthrone King Jesus over our bodies is by caring for our physical health. We must feed our bodies for health, which includes what we eat and how much we eat.[262] We must exercise our bodies for health.[263] And we must rest our bodies for health.[264] Taking care of your body honors King Jesus because you're partnering with him to fulfill his kingdom vision for your life.[265] Doing your part to maintain good health will allow you to complete the good works he's planned for you, both now, in your present service, and in your future.

Another kingdom truth to lay hold of is that exercising self-control over your physical appetites is a sign of Jesus's kingship.[266] Rather than allowing physical substances, like food, alcohol, or drugs, to rule over you, you are ruled by the Lord Jesus. You are governed by the Holy Spirit, not controlled by an addiction.

In multiple ways, seeking God's kingdom first requires distinctive physical lives, because our resident King is holy.[267]

Kingdom Key #5: Give King Jesus first place in your work. Most of our waking hours are devoted to our job, so it's crucial to embrace Jesus's reign over this vast territory of our lives. Let me outline two essential ways to do this.

First, realize that when you receive King Jesus, you get a new boss at work. Heaven's Majesty becomes your manager, so you now do your work for him.[268] Lay hold of that truth and it will surely change your attitude and work habits, especially if you feel like a slave at work!

Want to test whether King Jesus reigns over your work? If you're an employee, ask yourself whether your job performance makes your supervisor feel respected and well served. That's how you want your King to feel. If you're a manager, ask yourself whether your employees feel valued and well served. Remember that leadership in Jesus's kingdom is distinctively different. Jesus's reign is marked by a King who serves.[269]

Now get ready for a second way to crown King Jesus over your work, because it might rock your boat. Give Jesus the first part of your paycheck. Yes, throughout every era of kingdom history on Earth, a vital way for kingdom people to honor their Loving King is by giving back to him the first portion of their income, not the leftovers. Wisdom states it this way, "Honor the LORD with your wealth, with the first fruits of all your crops; then your barns will be filled to overflowing, and your vats will brim over with new wine."[270] Did you catch the promise of favor for obeying his Word? That's how the King reigns.

Your work becomes worship when you give cheerfully to King Jesus, with gratitude and faith.[271] Giving the first money from your paycheck pleases him because it shows your faith.[272] He is your Creator,[273] Sustainer,[274] Provider,[275] and the source of your prosperity.[276] Every good and perfect gift in your life comes from him.[277] All that you have comes from him.[278] By giving him the first and best of your income, you are declaring your faith in your Loving King. You're trusting him also to provide fully for any unexpected expenses that may come later in the pay period.

There's an essential truth to understand in this grace of giving, though. Please hear this. ***King Jesus doesn't need your money; he desires your heart.*** He created you to love you. He gave his life to draw you to him, so he could love you forever. And the one response he desires is the love of your heart.[279] By giving the first part of your paycheck to him, you're giving him your heart.

Jesus, himself, put it this way: "For where your treasure is, there your heart will be also."[280] Your checkbook or credit card statement is a leading indicator of your heart. The reason? You spend your money on what you value. So giving the first of your paycheck to King Jesus is a way of communicating that you value him first in your heart. You're giving him your heart, which is what he truly desires.

At the same time, you're loving him with your strength. That's because you devote your strength—your mental and physical energy—to your work, and your work produces your income. So you are giving King Jesus the gifts of your labor. Your grateful financial gifts rise up to give him pleasure and joy.[281]

When you honor King Jesus with your money, it opens the floodgates of his generosity toward you. Not so you can live a self-indulgent life, but so that you can serve him even more generously.[282] Let me also be straight with you about the flip side. If you reject King Jesus's reign over your work and wages, you dishonor him.[283] Your actions reveal your unbelieving rebellion in that territory of your life. You don't want to do that. You also forfeit the Generous King's favor over a significant part of your life. You can't afford to do that!

If you're wondering just how much of your paycheck you should give to King Jesus, I can't give you a specific number or percentage. Throughout the Scriptures, however, kingdom people are called to give generously. Israel was instructed to give ten percent (a tithe) of their income to the LORD. But they also gave a lot more than that through various gifts and offerings. Their covenant taught them to be generous—to God and to those in need. We should learn from their example.

King Jesus, himself, urges us to give generously. He is the extravagantly generous Giver, and he says, "Give, and it will be given to you. A good measure, pressed down, shaken together and running over, will be poured into your lap."[284] Many other New Testament scriptures also instruct us to be generous. So consider all of your God-given responsibilities, your values, and priorities. Then decide on a generous proportion of your income to give, first, to King Jesus. Give it cheerfully, and trust him to meet all your needs. Watch for his generosity toward you, so you can excel even more in the grace of giving.

Kingdom Key #6: Give King Jesus first place by serving people. When you receive King Jesus, you receive a new family and a new mission.[285] You are baptized by the Holy Spirit into his new community, the Church.[286] You're gifted by the Spirit to serve. You're drafted to play on the championship team that's advancing God's reign on Earth. You're given the opportunity to achieve greatness in God's kingdom.

King Jesus defines greatness as serving others.[287] He not only teaches us to serve others, he blazes a trail by giving us his own astonishing example.[288] Heaven's High King stoops to take up a towel and basin to wash his disciples' dirty feet. He ultimately gives everything (his life on the cross) to serve your needs and mine and to wash us clean from the dirt of our sin.

So why should you give King Jesus first place by serving others? Simply because he's worthy. He's your Servant King. He showed you the full extent of his love on the cross. Love so amazing, so divine, demands your heart, your life, your service.

Yet here's an encouraging truth: One of the reasons King Jesus wants you to serve is to flood your life with joy. Surprised? You shouldn't be. He's the life-giver. He's wired you so when you serve with your spiritual gifts, you'll benefit others and build up the church family. At the same time, you'll uncap inner springs of personal joy. If you're giving him the best of your service, you already know this. If you're not, what's holding you back from enthroning Jesus over this region of your life? Talk to your pastor or church leader and invest your gifts in serving the King by serving others.

Kingdom Key #7: Give King Jesus first place by representing him well.
King Jesus shines light and life into the darkness and disorder of this world. He did so in creation, and in forming Israel as his kingdom on Earth. Now he radiates his life-giving presence on this rebellious planet through you and me.[289]

There are only two kingdoms on Earth. People reside either in Satan's dominion of death, which leads to eternal judgment, banished from God's presence. Or they've been delivered into Christ's kingdom of love and eternal life, with a destiny in God's presence.[290] That leads us to a crucial kingdom key: the mission we've been given. We must give King Jesus first place by representing him well. He's the Loving King who rescues rebels and graciously grants them eternal life. He's building his Church,[291] and he wants to draw more people into his forever family. He doesn't want anyone to perish.[292] So he shines his loving, life-giving presence into the world, personally, through his family. People like you and me.

We extend King Jesus's reign when we seek to represent him well in our relationships with people who are still under Satan's domain of darkness. Folks who may have no idea that the King of the universe loves them with an overwhelming love. They remain captive to Satan's deceit, and are chained to his destiny of eternal death.

How do you represent King Jesus well? Follow his lead: live out his grace and truth.[293] Show people your King's love, with skin on. Declare his good news, with your words and with your actions. Pray and utilize your God-given abilities. Take advantage of some great resources to help you shine Christ's light into the world and in your relationships. Two of my favorites, *Becoming a Contagious Christian* and *Just Walk across the Room*, were written by Pastor Bill Hybels, a champion of the church being King Jesus's light to the world.[294]

There are few joys more exhilarating than experiencing the Holy Spirit working, through you, to draw another person to faith in King Jesus. There are few gifts more rewarding than knowing a person's eternal destiny has been changed from death to life because Heaven's Anointed King loved them into a relationship with himself, through his representative, you.

These seven kingdom keys are not complete in themselves, but they represent major landscapes of your life. As you read God's Word regularly, he will issue many commands to you relating to every region of your life. Your love for your King will be shown by obeying them, which will position every territory of your life to receive the goodness of his reign.

To wrap up, the throne room of the universe is issuing a royal summons to you: "Seek, first, King Jesus." Love him with all you've got.

How will you respond to God's Anointed King? I urge you to embrace his reign by obeying the seven kingdom keys. His kingdom will come, in your life, as it is in heaven. His reign will take hold on Earth, in your personal zip code. You'll position yourself to receive a greater measure of his goodness. God's Word reveals an unfailing truth: Where the King rules, he reigns with favor. Get ready to experience a fuller measure of life. The Lord Jesus wants to fill you.[295] He is the loving, life-giving King!

That brings us to the end of our 40 Day journey, but certainly not the end of the road walking with King Jesus. I trust that you have enjoyed traveling with His Majesty, and that you will press on, devoting yourself daily to your Awesome King.

I leave you with a blessing from God's Word.

> **The LORD invigorate you with the potency of life;**
> **the LORD smile upon you with generous favor;**
> **the LORD fill you with his presence,**
> **so that you overflow to others with his life-giving love.**[296]

[If you have benefited from *40 Days of God's Kingdom*, please write me a quick note to tell me how at www.40DaysofGodsKingdom.com Thanks.]

Appendix 1

I am deeply grateful for three formative influences that have shaped my life with personal devotions, each of which is woven into the fabric of this Appendix. During my first year of college, I was inspired by InterVarsity's profound booklet *Quiet Time,* a classic well worth reading. Professor Howard Hendricks rocked my world (and countless others) at Dallas Theological Seminary with his creative genius presenting the inductive method of studying God's Word. This simple process of observation, interpretation, and application allows the Holy Spirit to speak into our lives in order to produce life change. Thirdly, Pastor Wayne Cordeiro modeled building personal devotions effectively into the DNA of a church family. The New Hope movement of churches, founded by Pastor Wayne, has been mentored with a simple, yet profound method of journaling known by the acronym SOAP (Scripture, Observation, Application, Prayer). Pastor Wayne's book, *The Divine Mentor,* is an excellent resource for this devotional process. With gratitude for Pastor Wayne's leadership, we have simply revised the acronym to VINE, inspired by Jesus's imagery of the relationship in John 15.

V.I.N.E.

That the King of the universe would provide a way for us to know him is wonderful enough. But that **King Jesus actually desires our friendship**, that it gives him satisfaction, joy, and pleasure, truly boggles the mind.

God's Word declares that he created you to love you. He rescued you from Satan's death grip because he loves you. And he wants to spend the rest of your life and eternity loving you. Consider that it cost King Jesus the ultimate price, an agonizing death on the cross, to secure a relationship with you. It will make you humbly grateful for an indescribable gift, the gift of a forever friendship with the Loving King.

Take his words to heart.

> **I no longer call you a servant...**
> **Instead, I have called you my friend.**
> (John 15:15-16)

What kind of a friendship does Jesus desire to have with you? Again, hear his words.

> **I am the vine, you are the branches.**
> **When you're joined with me and I with you,**
> **the relation intimate,**
> **the harvest is sure to be abundant.**
> (John 15:5, The Message)

Think about Jesus's image of an orchard, "vine and branch." He envisions a relationship that is closely connected, life-giving, and life-changing. Like any friendship, the key to growth is sharing life by communicating with each other. How do we communicate with Heaven's King? Through two essential activities: he speaks to us through his Word and his Spirit; and we share our hearts with him through prayer.

The **V.I.N.E.** exercise is designed to help you grow a rich and rewarding friendship with King Jesus.

How to Connect with King Jesus through the V.I.N.E.

Step 1: Set a time
Like every other relationship, developing your friendship with Jesus requires spending time together. So set apart a regular, distraction-free, daily time to connect with Jesus through the *V.I.N.E.* You'll be glad you did!

Step 2: Set a place
Find a place that will be quiet and free from distractions. A regular place will help build a rhythm and habit in your devotional life of meeting with Jesus.

Step 3: Set your heart
Because you engage your friendship with King Jesus in your inner spirit, it's vital to meet him with three heart attitudes. Begin by praying to welcome him, and tune your heart in three ways:

1). *A quiet heart.*
"*Be still*, and know that I am God" (Psalm 46:10).

2). *An expectant heart.*
"*Open my eyes* to see wonderful things in your word" (Psalm 119:18).

3). *A responsive heart.*
"Now that you know these things, you will be blessed *if you do them*" (John 13:17).

A sample prayer to start with: "Dear Lord Jesus, it's wonderful to know that you're waiting to meet with me. Help me put aside all of the pressures and distractions of my day, and to focus on you. I want to hear your voice and experience your presence with me today. I open my heart to you now, and will do whatever you ask me to do. I know you love me and want the best for me."

Step 4: Read and Record

Read the two chapters from the daily Bible reading plan. As you read, underline or make note of anything the Lord impresses on you in a personal way.

Record your thoughts in response to the *V.I.N.E.* instructions below. Journaling allows you to process and focus your thoughts.

Verse: Write down the verse(s) that grab your attention, or seem especially important.

Insight: Write down, in your own words, what the verse(s) say.

Now what? Write down a specific way you need to apply this truth to your life.

Expression of prayer: Write your heart's response to Jesus. It may involve adoration, confession, thanksgiving, requests, etc.

As you embrace King Jesus, our True Vine, he will energize you and enrich your life with fruitfulness. You will receive a deeper measure of his life, which in turn will make his glory known (John 15:5, 8).

∞∞

A Sample V.I.N.E. Exercise

Date: **Bible Reading Plan:** Psalm 1, Mark 1

Verse(s): *What verse(s) speak especially to me?*

> Mark 1:35–37

Insight: *In my own words, what does the passage say?*

> As Jesus began preaching, healing, and calling people, he rose early in the morning to spend time with the Father. If Jesus devoted time for prayer with the Father, how much more should I?

Now what? *How, specifically, should I apply this to my life?*

> I will go to bed half an hour earlier, and set the alarm to get up thirty minutes earlier, in order to meet with the Lord Jesus. I will seek to hear his voice through reading the Bible and journal my response in prayer.

Expression of prayer: *What is my heart's response to Jesus?*

> Thank you, Lord Jesus, for coming into the world. Your miracles and teaching show me that you truly are Heaven's King. Amazing! Like those first fishermen, I want to follow you with all my heart. I know you came because you love me.

I need you in my life today. I need your love, your strength, and your wisdom to fill me and flow to my family and friends. Help me to be an encouragement today, especially to Malia. I love you and look forward to our times together. Thanks so much for your presence with me.

Appendix 2

V.I.N.E. Reading Plan for *40 Days of God's Kingdom*

- ☐ Day 1: Read *40 Days of God's Kingdom,* Introduction and Chapter 1
- ☐ Day 2: Genesis 1, Matthew 1
- ☐ Day 3: Genesis 2, Matthew 2
- ☐ Day 4: Genesis 3, Matthew 3
- ☐ Day 5: Genesis 4, Matthew 4
- ☐ Day 6: Genesis 5, Matthew 5
- ☐ Day 7: Sabbath rest

- ☐ Day 8: Read *40 Days of God's Kingdom*, Chapter 2
- ☐ Day 9: Genesis 12, Matthew 6
- ☐ Day 10: Genesis 22, Matthew 7
- ☐ Day 11: Exodus 20, Matthew 8
- ☐ Day 12: Exodus 40, Matthew 9
- ☐ Day 13: Deuteronomy 6, Matthew 10
- ☐ Day 14: Sabbath rest

- ☐ Day 15: Read *40 Days of God's Kingdom,* Chapter 3
- ☐ Day 16: 1 Samuel 8, Matthew 11
- ☐ Day 17: 1 Samuel 12, Matthew 12
- ☐ Day 18: 1 Samuel 16, Matthew 13
- ☐ Day 19: 2 Samuel 7, Matthew 14
- ☐ Day 20: 2 Kings 17, Matthew 15
- ☐ Day 21: Sabbath rest

- ☐ Day 22: Read *40 Days of God's Kingdom,* Chapter 4
- ☐ Day 23: Amos 2, Matthew 16
- ☐ Day 24: Amos 3, Matthew 17
- ☐ Day 25: Amos 5, Matthew 18
- ☐ Day 26: Amos 8, Matthew 19
- ☐ Day 27: Amos 9, Matthew 20
- ☐ Day 28: Sabbath rest

- ☐ Day 29: Read *40 Days of God's Kingdom,* Chapter 5
- ☐ Day 30: Psalm 8, Matthew 21
- ☐ Day 31: Psalm 16, Matthew 22
- ☐ Day 32: Psalm 21, Matthew 23
- ☐ Day 33: Psalm 33, Matthew 24
- ☐ Day 34: Proverbs 3, Matthew 25
- ☐ Day 35: Sabbath rest

- ☐ Day 36: Read *40 Days of God's Kingdom,* Chapter 6
- ☐ Day 37: Matthew 26, Ephesians 1
- ☐ Day 38: Matthew 27, Ephesians 2
- ☐ Day 39: Matthew 28, Ephesians 3
- ☐ Day 40: Acts 1, Ephesians 4
- ☐ Day 41: Acts 2, Ephesians 5
- ☐ Day 42: Sabbath rest

- ☐ Day 43: Read *40 Days of God's Kingdom,* Chapter 7 and Conclusion
- ☐ Day 44: Acts 3, Revelation 2
- ☐ Day 45: Acts 4, Revelation 5
- ☐ Day 46: Acts 5, Revelation 16
- ☐ Day 47: Acts 6, Revelation 19
- ☐ Day 48: Revelation 21–22
- ☐ Day 49: Sabbath rest

Endnotes

1. **Introduction**
   Kevin Fagan, "Gold Country Couple Discover $10 million in Buried Coins," *San Francisco Chronicle*, http://www.sfgate.com/news/article/Gold-Country-couple-discover-10-million-in-5266314.php.

2. Matthew uses the phrase "the kingdom of heaven" uniquely in the New Testament. The reference is synonymous with "the kingdom of God." In parallel passages in Mark and Luke, the latter expression is used. Matthew avoids using the sacred name of God by substituting the location of his throne, in keeping with his Jewish audience and flavor.

3. Matthew 13:44–46.

4. Matthew 12:28.

5. Matthew 26:29.

6. Romans 14:17.

7. Revelation 11:15.

8. In his classic work, George Eldon Ladd notes that the primary meaning of both the Hebrew word *malkuth* in the Old Testament and the Greek word *basileia* in the New Testament is the rank, authority, and sovereignty exercised by a king. *The Gospel of the Kingdom* (Grand Rapids, MI: Eerdmans, 1959), 19.

9. K. L. Schmidt, *Theological Dictionary of the New Testament*, 1:579–80. See also, Ladd, 19–23.

10. Bruce Waltke makes this distinction in Christopher W. Morgan and Robert A. Peterson, eds., *The Kingdom of God* (Wheaton, IL: Crossway, 2012), 49.

11. Ephesians 1:11.

12. Mark 1:15, Matthew 4:17. In Luke's portrait of Jesus, the Messiah launches his public ministry by claiming the fulfillment of Isaiah's prophecy concerning the Servant of the Lord in his mission (Luke 4:18–19). Yet Luke summarizes Jesus's message as "the good news of the kingdom of God" (Luke 4:43, 8:1, 16:16).

13. Acts 1:3.
14. Acts 17:11. These believers "received the message with great eagerness and examined the Scriptures every day to see if what Paul said was true."
15. 2 Timothy 3:16.
16. Countless preachers in this generation, including me, have been mentored by Haddon Robinson's genius that effective messages have one "Big Idea." See his book, *Biblical Preaching* (Grand Rapids, MI: Baker, 1980, 2001). My goal in this work is to present the big idea of the entire Bible.
17. Jesus affirms that he is central to Old Testament revelation (Luke 24:27; John 5:39).
18. Colossians 2:15.
19. Colossians 1:13–14.
20. Ephesians 1:9–10; Revelation 19–22.
21. Ephesians 1:6, 14.
22. Revelation 19:6–7.

Chapter 1
23. Genesis 1:26–8.
24. I am indebted to Bruce Waltke for this basic outline. For a full discussion of the exegetical issues and textual basis, see Waltke's series of articles in *Bibliotheca Sacra* 132 (1975): 25–36, 136–44, 216–28, 327–42; 133 (1976): 28–41.
25. John 1:1–2, 14.
26. Genesis 1:22, 28.
27. The plurality evident in Genesis 1:26 may indicate the fullness of majesty. But it also may hint at the plurality of Persons in the triune God, revealed in further Scripture as Father, Son, and Holy Spirit.
28. Genesis 1:26–27.
29. Genesis 1:12, 18, 20, 25.
30. Genesis 1:31.
31. Psalm 19:1–6.
32. Genesis 1:29–30, 2:8–9.

33.   Genesis 2:15–25.
34.   Genesis 2:16–17.
35.   Deuteronomy 6:4–9; John 14:15, 21, 23.
36.   Genesis 3:1–7.
37.   Ephesians 2:2.
38.   Genesis 2:17.
39.   Genesis 3:8–19.
40.   Genesis 3:14. Dust, the serpent's food, is a symbol of death in 3:19.
41.   Romans 8:19–21.
42.   Genesis 3:20.
43.   Genesis 3:15.
44.   Genesis 3:21.
45.   Hebrews 10:10–14.
46.   Genesis 3:22–24.
47.   Genesis 4:1–16.
48.   Genesis 4:19–24.
49.   Genesis 5:1–32.
50.   Genesis 5:24.
51.   Genesis 6:1–8.
52.   Genesis 6:5.
53.   Genesis 6:8.
54.   Genesis 9:1–17.
55.   Genesis 9:18–28.
56.   Genesis 11:1–9.

Chapter 2

57.   John 14:30; Ephesians 2:2.
58.   Genesis 12:1–3, 15:9–21, 17:1–27.
59.   Note Genesis 1:22, 28.
60.   King Jesus affirms this purpose in John 10:10.
61.   John 10:10, 20:31.
62.   Genesis 17:8–9.
63.   Romans 4:11.

64. Ephesians 2:8–9.
65. Genesis 15:6; Romans 3:21–24, 4:1–3.
66. For example, God protects his promise to give Abraham descendants when the patriarch's fear for his life results in Sarai being taken into the harem of other men (Genesis 12:10–20; 20:1–18).
67. For example, God protects Jacob from the hostility of Laban (Genesis 31:22–25) and the possible attack of Esau (Genesis 32:1–21; 33:1–20). He also moves the family to Egypt to ensure their survival during a famine (Genesis 45:16–46:30).
68. Exodus 1–18.
69. Each of the catastrophic judgments is directed at the idols Egypt worshiped. See John F. Walvoord and Roy B. Zuck, eds., *The Bible Knowledge Commentary* (Wheaton, IL: Victor Books, 1985), 120.
70. Exodus 3:14–15.
71. John 10:11.
72. John 14:6.
73. John 11:25.
74. John 8:58.
75. Exodus 19–24.
76. Exodus 19:4–6.
77. At the heart of the Covenant are the Ten Commandments (Exodus 20:1–17). The first four commandments are devoted to loving God and the last six are devoted to loving people.
78. Exodus 25–40.
79. Leviticus 1–10.
80. Genesis 2:16–17.
81. Leviticus 11–27.
82. Leviticus 11:44–45, 19:2, 20:26.
83. Numbers 1:1–10:10.
84. Numbers 10:11–22:1.
85. Numbers 22:2–36:13.
86. Deuteronomy 1:2–3.

87.   Numbers 13:1–14:45.
88.   Deuteronomy 34:10–12.
89.   Deuteronomy 4:37, 7:7, 10:15, 23:5, 32:10–14.
90.   Deuteronomy 6:4–6, 7:9, 11:13, 19:8–9.
91.   Matthew 22:34–38; Mark 12:28–30.

Chapter 3

92.   Matthew 1:17 reflects this flow in Israel's history.
93.   Joshua 24.
94.   Judges 17:6, 21:25.
95.   This pattern, typical in the narrative of the book, is observable in the
       first Judge, Othniel: apostasy (3:7b); oppression (3:8); distress (3:9a);
       deliverance (3:9b–10).
96.   1 Samuel 11:14–12:25, note 12:14–15.
97.   Exodus 34:6.
98.   Leviticus 26:33; Deuteronomy 28:64.
99.   Jeremiah 29:10.
100.   2 Chronicles 36:22–33.
101.   These acts of election include: (1) the tribe of Levi is chosen to serve be-
       fore the ark of the covenant (1 Chronicles 15:2, 23:24–32); (2) David
       is chosen to be king over all of Israel (1 Chronicles 28:4; 2 Chronicles
       6:6); (3) Solomon is chosen to be king and to build the temple (1
       Chronicles 28:5–6, 10; 29:1); (4) Jerusalem is chosen to be the holy
       city, the location of the King's throne (2 Chronicles 6:6, 34, 38; 12:13
       33:7); and (5) the temple is chosen to be the place where God's Name
       would be present among his people (2 Chronicles 7:12,16; 33:7).
102.   1 Chronicles 28:7; 2 Chronicles 6:16, 7:17, 12:1, 33:8.
103.   1 Samuel 8.
104.   2 Samuel 7; 1 Chronicles 17; 2 Chronicles 13:5, 21:7, 23:3; Psalm
       89:3–4.
105.   Luke 1:32–33.
106.   Revelation 21:2–3, 9–26.

Chapter 4

107. 2 Chronicles 20:20.
108. Jehoram (2 Chronicles 21:12–19); Joash (2 Chronicles 24:19–25); Amaziah (2 Chronicles 25:15–16, 20); Manasseh (2 Chronicles 33:10–11). See 2 Chronicles 36:15–16.
109. Ezekiel 3:17, 33:7.
110. The dates of Obadiah's and Joel's lives are debated. I list them as preexilic prophets.
111. Amos 4:13; 5:8; 9:5–6.
112. Job 38:1–42:6.
113. For example, Psalm 47.
114. For example, Psalm 45, 110.
115. For example, Psalm 84.
116. For example, Psalm 120–134.
117. For example, Psalm 113.
118. Psalm 33.
119. Psalm 29.
120. Psalms 8, 19, 104.
121. For example, Psalm 30, 34.
122. For example, Psalms 1, 49.
123. For example, Psalm 51, 142.
124. Proverbs 1:2–6.
125. Proverbs 9:10.
126. There are two component parts to "the fear of the LORD": (1) God's revealed truth (cf., 2 Kings 17:24–28; Psalm 19:7–9); and (2) an attitude of reverence or awe for the LORD that leads to obedience (Proverbs 1:7).
127. Ecclesiastes 12:13.
128. John 1:14.
129. Hebrews 1:1–3.
130. Colossians 2:3.

Chapter 5

131. Matthew 1:1
132. Galatians 3:16.
133. Luke 1:32–33.
134. Matthew 2:2.
135. Matthew 21:43, 28:18–20.
136. Mark 10:45.
137. Luke 3:38.
138. Luke 19:10.
139. John 1:1–14.
140. John 20:31.
141. Matthew 1:23; Luke 1:26–35.
142. Mark 1:15; Matthew 4:17.
143. Matthew 13:1–52, 21:28–22:14; Mark 4:1–34; Luke 8:4–18.
144. Mark 1:22.
145. John 14:6.
146. Mark 4:35–5:43.
147. Mark 1:15; Luke 4:43.
148. Romans 5:8; 1 John 4:9–10.
149. 1 John 2:2.
150. 1 Corinthians 15:35–57.
151. Romans 1:4.
152. Genesis 3:15.
153. 1 John 3:8.
154. Colossians 2:15; 1 Corinthians 15:54–56.
155. Colossians 1:13–14.
156. 1 Corinthians 15:20.
157. Romans 16:20; Colossians 2:13–15.
158. John 3:16; I Corinthians 15:55–56.
159. Matthew 1:1; John 10:10, 20:31; Galatians 3:16.
160. Matthew 26:17–29; Mark 14:12–25; 1 Corinthians 5:7, 11–24.

161.   Matthew 5:17.
162.   Romans 4:25; Hebrews 10:10; 1 John 2:2.
163.   1 Corinthians 6:11; Ephesians 5:25–26; Titus 3:5; Hebrews 10:22.
164.   John 6:35, 51; 1 Corinthians 11:23–24; 1 John 1:4.
165.   John 1:9, 12:4, 6; 2 Corinthians 4:4, 6.
166.   Romans 8:34; Hebrews 7:25.
167.   Matthew 27:51; Hebrews 9:3, 8; 10:19–20.
168.   Romans 3:25; 1 John 2:2.
169.   Ephesians 5:2; Hebrews 9:14, 10:5–7.
170.   Hebrews 10:5–7.
171.   Ephesians 2:14–18; Colossians 1:20.
172.   2 Corinthians 5:21; Ephesians 1:7; 1 John 2:2.
173.   Isaiah 53:10.
174.   Leviticus 23:5–43.
175.   John 1:1, 14; Hebrews 1:1–3.
176.   Hebrews 4:14–5:10; 8:1–10:18.
177.   Luke 1:32.
178.   1 Corinthians 11:25.
179.   Colossians 2:3.
180.   Matthew 21:31.
181.   Luke 11:20.
182.   Matthew. 25:31–34.
183.   Mark 14:25.
184.   Matthew 24:42–25:46.

Chapter 6

185.   Ephesians 2:11–22, 3:2–12.
186.   Ephesians 3:10.
187.   1 Timothy 2:5.
188.   Matthew 26:26–28.
189.   Matthew 5:17.
190.   Colossians 2:14.

191. Romans 7:6; Galatians 3:24–25.
192. Romans 8:4; Galatians 3:16–26.
193. 1 Samuel 16:13–14; Psalm 51:11.
194. Acts 2:1–13.
195. Ephesians 1:13–14, 4:30.
196. Romans 8:16.
197. John 16:13; 1 John 2:27.
198. Romans 8:14.
199. Romans 8:26.
200. Romans 8:2; 2 Corinthians 3:8–9, 17.
201. 2 Corinthians 3:18.
202. Acts 1:8.
203. Romans 5:5; Ephesians 3:16–19.
204. 1 Corinthians 12:1–31.
205. Galatians 5:22–23.
206. Romans 8:16–17.
207. 1 Corinthians 2:9.
208. Matthew 20:18–20. Each Gospel writer records Jesus commissioning his disciples. Matthew's account is the most comprehensive.
209. 1 Corinthians 12:13.
210. John 8:12.
211. Matthew 5:14.
212. Ephesians 2:6, 10.
213. Colossians 1:27.
214. John 15:1–8.
215. 1 Corinthians 12:1–31.
216. John 17:20–23; Ephesians 4:1–16.
217. John 13:34.
218. Mark 12:28–31.
219. John 13:35.
220. 1 Corinthians 13:1–3.
221. Ephesians 2:20.

Chapter 7

222.   Revelation 1–3.
223.   Revelation 4–20.
224.   Revelation 21–22.
225.   Revelation 1:9–20.
226.   Revelation 2–3.
227.   Revelation 1:17–18.
228.   Revelation 4–20.
229.   Revelation 4–5.
230.   Revelation 2:13.
231.   Revelation 5:6. "Seven horns": the number seven represents completeness or perfection, and horns symbolize power. Together they symbolize perfect power.
232.   "Seven eyes": the number seven, again, represents completeness or perfection, and the eyes symbolize what is seen. Together they symbolize perfect sight.
233.   Revelation 5:9–14.
234.   Revelation 6–16.
235.   Revelation 15:3–4.
236.   Revelation 16:5, 7.
237.   Revelation 7:10.
238.   Revelation 9:20–21.
239.   Revelation 16:9–11.
240.   Revelation 17–18.
241.   Revelation 19:1–10.
242.   Revelation 19:11–16.
243.   Revelation 19:17–20:15. Different interpretations of end time events, such as Christ's millennial reign on Earth, shouldn't obscure the major truths of Christ's return in glory to judge and to rule.
244.   Revelation 21:1–22:5.
245.   John 17:3.
246.   Revelation 11:15.
247.   Revelation 22:17.

Conclusion

248.   Matthew 6:33.

249.   1 John 1:9.

250.   John1:12.

251.   Galatians 5:22–23.

252.   John 13:34.

253.   Ephesians 5:21–33; 1 Peter 3:7.

254.   Ephesians 6:1–3.

255.   Ephesians 6:4.

256.   Deuteronomy 6:4–9.

257.   Ephesians 5:1–14.

258.   Matthew 5:44; Luke 6:27.

259.   Romans 5:8.

260.   1 Corinthians 6:19–20.

261.   1 Corinthians 6:16–18; Matthew 5:27–28.

262.   Proverbs 23:2, 23:20–21, 28:7; Titus 1:12.

263.   1 Timothy 4:8.

264.   Genesis 2:2; Exodus 20:8–11; Psalm 127:2; Mark 2:27–28.

265.   Ephesians 2:10.

266.   Ephesians 5:18; Galatians 5:22–23.

267.   1 Peter 1:15–16.

268.   Ephesians 6:5–9; Colossians 3:22–25.

269.   Mark 10:45, John 13:1–17.

270.   Proverbs 3:9–10.

271.   2 Corinthians 9:7.

272.   Hebrews 11:6.

273.   Psalm 139:13.

274.   Hebrews 1:3.

275.   Psalm 23:1.

276.   Deuteronomy 8:18.

277.   James 1:17.

278.   1 Corinthians 4:7.

279.   Mark 12:29–30.

280. Matthew 6:21.
281. Philippians 4:18–19.
282. 2 Corinthians 9:6–11.
283. Malachi 3:7–12.
284. Luke 6:38.
285. Matthew 28:18–20.
286. 1 Corinthians 12:13.
287. Mark 10:43–45.
288. John 13:1–17.
289. Matthew 5:14; Acts 1:8.
290. Matthew 25:31–46.
291. Matthew 16:18.
292. 2 Peter 3:9.
293. John 1:14.
294. Bill Hybels and Mark Mittelburg, *Becoming A Contagious Christian* (Grand Rapids, MI: Zondervan, 1994). Bill Hybels, *Just Walk Across the Room* (Grand Rapids, MI: Zondervan, 2006).
295. John 10:10.
296. Adapted from Numbers 6:24–26.